Volume 1

A-BOMB

ARCHAEOLOGICAL
TECHNIQUES

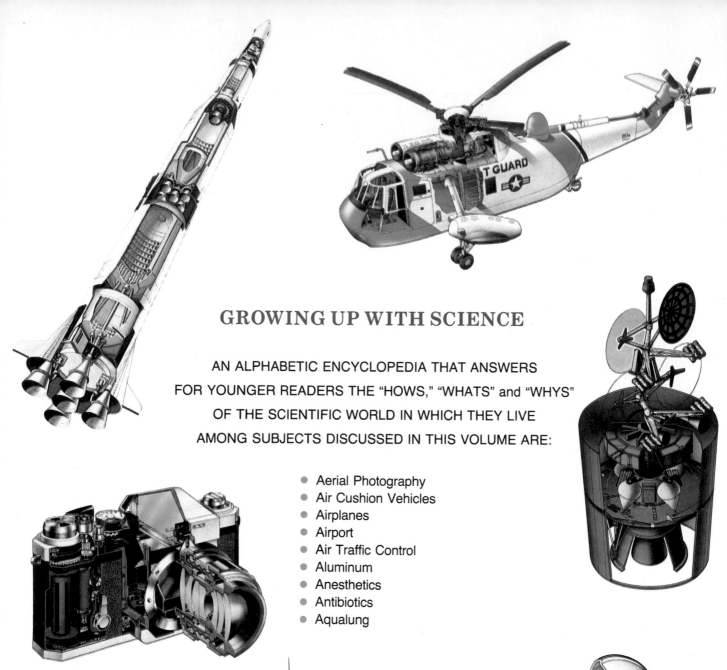

GROWING UP WITH SCIENCE

AN ALPHABETIC ENCYCLOPEDIA THAT ANSWERS
FOR YOUNGER READERS THE "HOWS," "WHATS" and "WHYS"
OF THE SCIENTIFIC WORLD IN WHICH THEY LIVE
AMONG SUBJECTS DISCUSSED IN THIS VOLUME ARE:

- Aerial Photography
- Air Cushion Vehicles
- Airplanes
- Airport
- Air Traffic Control
- Aluminum
- Anesthetics
- Antibiotics
- Aqualung

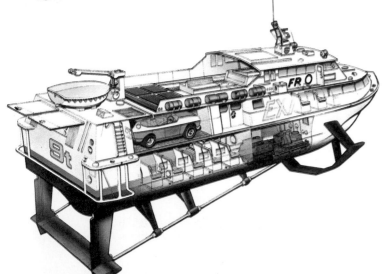

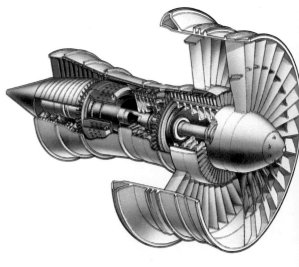

THE ILLUSTRATED ENCYCLOPEDIA OF
INVENTION

VOLUME
1

H. S. STUTTMAN, INC. *publishers*   Westport, Connecticut 06889

EXECUTIVE EDITOR

MICHAEL DEMPSEY Author and publisher specializing in science-based information books for children, including the *Understanding Science* series. Joint founder of children's publishers *Grisewood & Dempsey*.

MAJOR CONTRIBUTORS

JOHN PATON Author and editor on a wide range of children's books with particular emphasis on astronomy and science. *Finding Out Children's Encyclopedia, Knowledge Encyclopedia, Children's Encyclopedia of Science, Atoms and Energy, Stars and Planets.*

KEITH WICKS Author of many children's books on science and technology, and contributor of encyclopedia articles for major international publishers. *Purnell's Pictorial Encyclopedia, Encyclopedia of Nature and Science, Science Can Be Fun, All Color Book of Science Facts, World of Knowledge, Inventions-Macmillan Color Library.*

ROBIN KERROD Fellow of the Royal Astronomical Society lecturer, author of over fifty scientific books for children. *Purnell's Concise Encyclopedia of Science, Purnell's Dictionary of Science.*

KEITH LYE Fellow of the Royal Geographic Society, author of many earth science books, including the *Caxton Atlas of the Earth, Planet Earth, Rocks and Minerals, Countries of the World.*

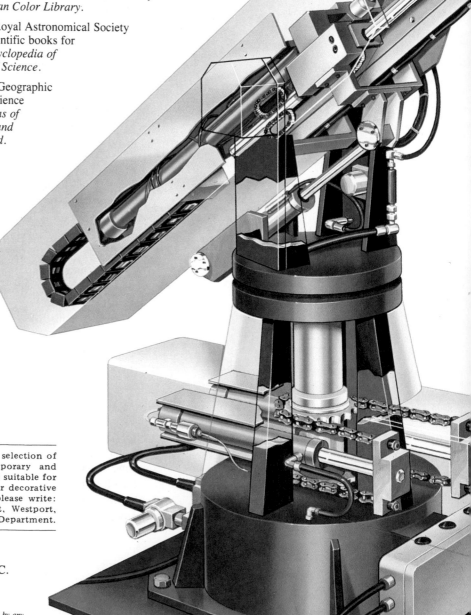

EDITORIAL STAFF

Series Editors
Fran Jones, U.K.
Elaine Landry, U.S.

Senior Editors
Nina Shandloff
Paul Berman

Art Directors
Edward Pitcher
Chris Legee

Production Managers
Dennis Hovell
Steve Roberts

Publishing Coordinator
Terry Waters

Published by H. S. STUTTMAN INC.
Westport, Connecticut 06889
© Marshall Cavendish Limited 1987

3P (1229) 65–190

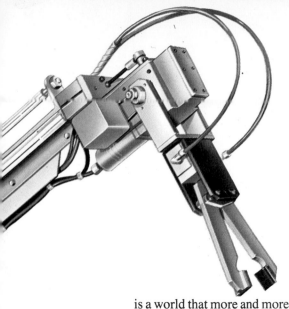

Introduction

GROWING UP WITH SCIENCE has been written and published especially for children, so that they can learn all about the fascinating and challenging world of science. It is a world that more and more over the ages, and especially in this 20th century, has come to affect so much of our lives. It is involved with the way we eat and the way we travel, the homes we live in and the clothes we wear, how we become ill and how medicine can make us better, and has given us fantastic means of communicating and exploring.

Because science will be around us even more in the future, tomorrow's adults must start learning today to be ready to take their places in this computerized, transistorized, antibiotic, nuclear, supersonic age!

Machines, manufacturing and other processes, scientific discoveries and techniques, structures, devices galore ... as well as the natural phenomena of our universe, from atoms and molecules to the solar system ... are discussed in VOLUMES 1 through 22. Topics are in alphabetical order, the specially written texts accompanied on every page by dynamic, full-color photographs, drawings, and diagrams that **show** what is being described. They make up a remarkable journey with the people and ideas that have made our modern world and all its wonders.

Descriptions of the major INVENTIONS that brought humanity from living in caves to walking in space ... everything from the origins of the wheel, the telescope, and printing ... to plastics, radar, and nuclear power ... fill all of VOLUME 23. In addition to the learning experience, think of what a convenient source this is when dates, names, and facts are needed for school.

BIOGRAPHIES of the outstanding people who made these changes possible are in VOLUME 24. From Roger Bacon, the 13th-century British philosopher and scientist ... to Chester Carlson, the ingenious American who invented the photocopying process called xerography; from Blaise Pascal, the 17th-century Frenchman who, among other things, constructed the first working calculating machine ... to Enrico Fermi, the brilliant Italian physicist who discovered how to split the atom ... and so many more!

To top off this great store of exciting and useful information, VOLUME 25 contains 91 SCIENCE PROJECTS to be performed at home to see scientific happenings at first hand! In VOLUME 26, a GLOSSARY explains the difficult words (printed in small capital letters in the texts), and an INDEX gives the location of whatever the reader wants to know about ... so there is never a delay in the exciting process of **growing up with science** for a better place in tomorrow's world!

A-Bomb

The A-bomb, or atomic bomb, is a weapon of tremendous power. It has been used only twice in war. In 1945 World War II was finally brought to an end when the United States dropped atomic bombs on the cities of Hiroshima and Nagasaki in Japan.

Nuclear fission
All the substances around us are made up of tiny particles called atoms. The center of an atom is called the nucleus. If a nucleus is split into smaller particles, a great deal of energy is released.

This process is called nuclear fission. Even a small piece of material contains millions of atoms. So, if it is made to undergo nuclear fission, an enormous amount of energy is released. This is what gives the atomic bomb its tremendous power.

Most natural substances have atoms with nucleii that are extremely difficult to split. There is one exception—the metal uranium. Its relatively large atoms do not hold together as firmly as those of other natural substances.

The structure of atoms
In order to understand nuclear fission, we must think about the structure of atoms. All atoms are made up in the same way. Tiny particles called ELECTRONS circle (orbit) around the nucleus, like planets moving around the sun. A hydrogen atom has a nucleus with just one particle called a proton. All other atoms have nucleii with both PROTONS and NEUTRONS. Each element (simple substance) has a different number of protons in the nucleii of its atoms. However, the number of neutrons may vary. Atoms of the same element, but with different numbers of neutrons, are called ISOTOPES.

Isotopes
To tell the difference between isotopes, scientists often use the chemical symbol for the element, followed by the number of particles in the nucleus. For example, the three naturally occurring isotopes of uranium are referred to as U-238, U-235 and U-234. Each of these isotopes has 92 protons in each atom. But U-238 also has 146 neutrons (92+146=238), whereas U-235 has 143 neutrons, and U-234 has 142 neutrons.

This difference in the number of neutrons gives rise to some different physical properties. In particular, unlike the other natural uranium isotopes, U-235 can be split. In other words, the nucleii of its atoms can be split up to release nuclear (atomic) energy. For this reason, U-235 is the isotope which is used in the atomic bomb.

The chain reaction
Uranium and certain other heavy elements are naturally RADIOACTIVE. That is, they emit energy in the form of radiation and change into other elements. Over a period of several thousand years, some of the atoms in a piece of uranium will change into lead. In the atomic bomb, this change is made to happen extremely quickly. The vast energy thus released is in the form

The results of any kind of nuclear attack have been so terrible that thousands of people all over the world now gather together at demonstrations. They want to let the politicians know that they never want bombs to be used in war again. Here is a peaceful demonstration being held in Washington, D.C.

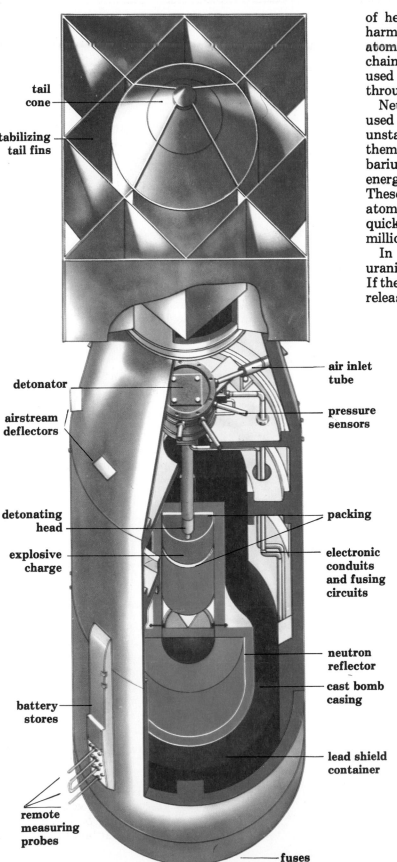

tail cone

stabilizing tail fins

detonator

airstream deflectors

detonating head

explosive charge

battery stores

remote measuring probes

air inlet tube

pressure sensors

packing

electronic conduits and fusing circuits

neutron reflector

cast bomb casing

lead shield container

fuses

of heat and GAMMA RADIATION, which is extremely harmful to life. The process by which the uranium atoms are made to release energy rapidly is called a chain reaction. The fission (splitting) of one nucleus is used to start the fission of other nucleii, and so on throughout the mass of uranium.

Neutrons moving at almost the speed of light are used to blast the nucleii of U-235 atoms. These are so unstable that a blow from a single neutron will split them. Usually, two smaller atoms of elements such as barium and krypton are formed. In addition to the energy released, two or three neutrons are let out. These fly out so fast that they split other uranium atoms. The process thus continues, and it happens so quickly that all the uranium atoms are split within one-millionth of a second.

In practice, there has to be a certain amount of uranium present before the chain reaction can carry on. If there is less than this amount, too few of the neutrons released will hit other atoms, so the reaction will not

Left: A cutaway view of the U-235 atomic bomb "Little Boy," which was dropped on Hiroshima in 1945.

Below: The chain reaction that produced the power. One neutron strikes a U-235 atom. This turns into U-236, which splits, releasing more neutrons to continue the reaction.

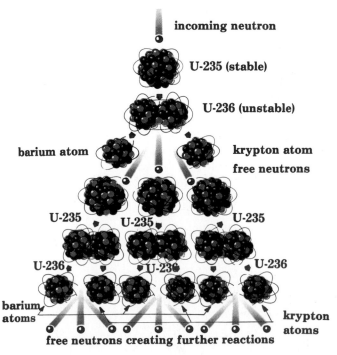

incoming neutron

U-235 (stable)

U-236 (unstable)

barium atom

krypton atom

free neutrons

U-235

U-235

U-235

U-236

U-236

U-236

barium atoms

krypton atoms

free neutrons creating further reactions

build up as it should. The minimum amount of material needed to make sure that a chain reaction takes place is called the CRITICAL MASS.

Atomic bomb design

Nuclear fuel is just one small part of the atomic bomb. Complex equipment is needed to set it off. Reliable safety devices are also used so that it will not go off by accident. In the case of uranium, a piece larger than the critical mass would explode immediately. So this fuel has to be inserted in two or more pieces. These are kept a safe distance apart until the bomb is to be set off. Then the pieces are brought together to start the chain reaction. Sometimes a device that looks like a gun is used to fire one piece of uranium at another. The gun is fired by means of an ordinary explosive charge. The resulting impact welds the two pieces of uranium together to form one piece heavier than the critical mass. The nuclear explosion follows instantly.

Atomic bombs using plutonium fuel are more complicated. The pieces of plutonium have to be combined extremely quickly or they will not explode properly. It is difficult to make a gun-type device combine the plutonium pieces at a high enough speed. A technique called IMPLOSION is used instead. Several wedge-shaped pieces of plutonium are arranged around a source of neutrons. This neutron source is essential to ensure a fast chain reaction in plutonium. To set off the bomb, charges behind the wedges are detonated (made to explode) together. This forces the wedges together to form a ball, which immediately undergoes a chain reaction.

The explosives used to start the chain reaction can be set off in various ways. In 1945, atomic bombs containing ALTIMETERS were dropped over Japan. The altimeters were set to detonate the bombs when they had fallen to a certain height above the ground. This ensured the maximum effect.

Developing the bomb

On August 2nd 1939, the scientist Albert Einstein wrote to Franklin D. Roosevelt, who was then the President of the United States. In his letter, Einstein pointed out that the Germans were trying to build an atomic bomb. With the world on the verge of war, Roosevelt realized the importance of his country building an atomic bomb before Germany. As a result, the United States Government set up the Manhattan Project. The aim of this project was simply to make an atomic bomb as soon as possible.

The principle behind the bomb had been understood for some time. However, it was difficult to find enough nuclear fuel for even one bomb, because only about 0.7 percent of natural uranium consists of the necessary isotope U-235. The rest is mainly U-238. So about 50 tons of pure uranium would be needed to give enough

Above: An enormous mushroom-shaped cloud forms as an experimental British atomic bomb explodes at Maralinga, Australia.

U-235 to make one atomic bomb. To obtain this amount of uranium, about 25,000 tons of ORE would have to be refined. In fact, this process was fairly simple. The main problem was getting the U-235 isotope out of the pure metal. This could not be done by ordinary chemical means because all isotopes of a substance behave in the same way in chemical reactions. The only possible way of separating the isotopes was by weight. Eventually, suitable techniques were developed for producing "enriched" uranium—that is, uranium consisting mainly of U-235. Meanwhile, others were looking for ways of obtaining plutonium fuel.

Plutonium occurs naturally, but only in minute amounts. To obtain enough for use in a bomb, the metal had to be manufactured from uranium in a nuclear reactor. This was finally done, and the plutonium was used to fuel the first atomic bomb.

Today, the atomic bomb is used as a trigger to set off the even more powerful hydrogen bomb.

See also: BOMBS, EXPLOSIVES, NUCLEAR REACTOR

Abrasives

We all use abrasives of some kind every day. We clean our teeth with toothpaste, wo sandpaper paintwork, we use scouring cloth to remove some rust or polish a metal, we clean out the bathtub with scouring powder. In all these actions we are using an abrasive.

Abrasives are hard substances that are used for grinding, smoothing, polishing or cleaning other substances that are usually softer than the abrasive. Abrasives are used in three main ways.

One way is to use the abrasive material directly on a substance; sharpening a knife on a grinding wheel or on a stone is an example of this.

Another way is to coat a substance such as stiff paper, cloth or the surface of a wheel with grains of abrasive material, and use this as a tool; sandpaper and scouring cloth are examples of this.

The third way is to mix abrasive particles with a powerful blast of air and direct the blast at stone or glass to clean or cut it. This is called sandblasting. It is often used to clean the outside of buildings.

Different abrasives

Some abrasives are made from minerals found in the earth, such as sand, quartz, corundum and diamonds. Others are man-made and include SYNTHETIC diamonds, silicon carbide (a mixture of sand and coke melted and crushed) and alumina (crystals of bauxite).

The size of the particles in an abrasive determines what it will be used for. Abrasives with large particles are used for cutting and grinding. Those with small particles are used for polishing.

Using abrasives

Abrasives are used in the making of most things we see around us. All the parts of an automobile engine have to be cleaned and ground to exact sizes before being put together. This is done by grinding the parts with abrasives to smooth the rough castings. Industrial tools are cut to shape and kept sharp by using abrasives.

Most industrial abrasives are used in the form of grinding wheels. The tiny particles of abrasive are sunk into clay or resin which is then hardened by baking in a kiln. There are grinding wheels of all shapes and sizes. They can be tiny wheels used to fashion jewelry, or huge wheels several feet in diameter used to shape 20-ton steel bars. Narrow grinding wheels, turning at very high speed, cut through the hardest metals. These wheels are often coated with diamond dust. Diamond, the hardest known natural substance, is used a great deal in grinding and cutting. Steel drills studded with diamonds are used to drill through hard rock.

Moving belts coated with abrasives are now being

Below: Sand-blasting is a technique used to clean buildings. This picture shows a workman cleaning the London Law Courts. The dirt on this building was up to 2 inches (5 centimeters) thick in some places. The abrasive used is made from crushed rock. Compressed air is used to blow the sand through the nozzle of a hose.

used more and more in industry. These belts are made of strong cloth or plastic, and can be coated with almost any abrasive.

See also: CRYSTALS, DIAMOND, STONECUTTING

Accelerators, particle

Particle accelerators are machines used to fire particles smaller than atoms at extremely high speeds. These fast-moving particles may be used to split atoms. Sometimes, the particles are made to combine with atoms. In both cases, new substances may be formed.

Uses of accelerators

Nuclear scientists use huge accelerators to study the behavior of atoms and the particles from which they are made. The first experiments with accelerators were designed to probe the center, or nucleus, of the atom. As the nucleus was split in the process, the machines became known as "atom smashers." But "nucleus smashers" would have been a better name. For smashing an atom is a simple matter that does not require an accelerator.

The outer parts of atoms consist of particles called ELECTRONS, and these are quite easy to remove. Just giving a body a positive electric charge will remove some of the electrons from its atoms. But the nucleus of an atom consists of particles called PROTONS and NEUTRONS bound tightly together. This is why the nucleus must be bombarded by fast-moving particles if it is to be changed in any way.

The nature of a simple substance, or element, is determined by the structure of its nucleii. This is why bombarding a nucleus can cause a new element to be formed. For centuries, scientists had tried to turn common metals into gold, but without success. With an accelerator, this process, called TRANSMUTATION, is now possible. Unfortunately, the cost of operating an accelerator would be much greater than the value of the gold.

Over the years, the power of accelerators has been greatly increased. The most powerful types can fire particles at such great speeds that some of their energy creates new particles when they strike their target. This is in accordance with Einstein's statement that energy and mass are interchangeable.

Linear accelerators

A linear accelerator moves particles in straight lines. It is the simplest type of accelerator, and can take various forms. Some are as long as 2 miles (3 kilometers). One type of linear accelerator consists of a cylinder containing a series of hollow metal tubes (drift tubes) arranged in a straight line. Protons or electrons are passed in at one end of the cylinder. These sub-atomic particles are electrically charged so other charges will attract or repel them. Opposite charges attract each other, and like charges repel.

A proton, for example, has a positive charge and will be attracted by negative charges and repelled by positive charges. In the accelerator, a device called a KLYSTRON produces a rapidly changing electric field that passes along the walls of the cylinder. Each part of the cylinder is given a negative charge and then a positive charge.

The system is arranged so that a particle entering the cylinder is first attracted by an opposite electric charge on the walls in front of it. This makes it go faster (accelerate). The field then changes, and would stop the

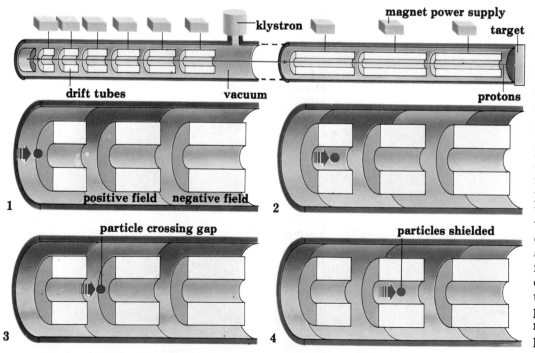

Left: A linear particle accelerator. The particles are accelerated by a changing electric field set up by a klystron. (1) A proton enters the tube and is accelerated by the negative field. (2) The proton is shielded from the positive field that would otherwise slow it down. (3) The proton is again accelerated by a negative field. (4) It is once more shielded when the positive field is present. This process repeats, giving the proton a high speed.

motion of the particle. But by this time, the particle is shielded from the field by the first drift tube, so the particle continues unhindered. When it emerges from the drift tube, an opposite field is again in front of it, so it is accelerated once more. All along the cylinder, the particle is accelerated each time it is exposed. The more it accelerates, the farther it travels while the field changes. So the drift tubes are made progressively longer. This arrangement ensures that the particle remains shielded until the field is again favorable.

In practice, a stream of particles is fired along the cylinder. Magnets are used to keep the particles close together, so that they form a narrow beam. This smashes into the target at the far end of the cylinder.

Circular accelerators

In circular accelerators, the particles pass the same accelerating devices many times. So it is easier to accelerate the particles to high speeds. In the CYCLOTRON type, particles are fed in at the gap between two semi-circular (D-shaped) plates. An alternating electric field and a fixed magnetic field make the particles accelerate in a spiral path.

In the SYNCHRO-CYCLOTRON, the electric field is made to change in step with the particles crossing between the plates. This produces a faster final speed. The SYNCHROTRON is even more powerful. It has magnets that vary in strength. These keep the particles moving in a circle until they have reached the desired speed.

See also: ATOMS AND MOLECULES, MAGNETISM

Above: A device called an intersecting storage ring (ISR). The ISR makes it possible to watch what happens when high-energy protons collide.

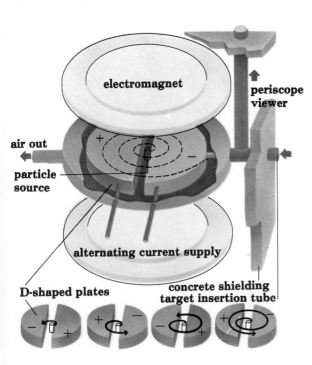

Left: In the cyclotron, particles are released between the D-shaped plates. A fixed magnetic field from the electromagnet and a changing electric field between the plates both influence the particles. As a result, they accelerate in a widening spiral path.

Right: The synchrotron accelerates particles injected into a vacuum tube. Powerful electromagnets guide the particles into a circular path. They accelerate to reach high speeds.

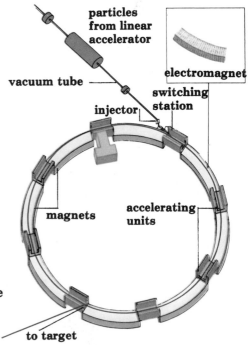

Accelerometer

An accelerometer is an instrument for measuring acceleration—the rate at which a vehicle gathers speed. There are two main types of accelerometer. One measures linear (straight-line) acceleration. The other type measures angular (turning) acceleration.

Linear accelerometers

The linear accelerometer has many uses in the motor industry. It is used to measure the forward ACCELERATION of a car—that is, the rate at which it gathers speed. The accelerometer can also measure the reverse effect—DECELERATION. This happens when the brakes of a car are applied. The reading on the accelerometer is, therefore, an indication of how well the brakes work. Another use of the linear accelerometer is to measure the up-and-down accelerations caused by bumpy roads. Vibrations in ships and aircraft can also be measured by the accelerometer.

The linear accelerometer usually contains a weight that can move in a straight line called the sensitive AXIS. The weight pushes against a spring. When the instrument is accelerated in the direction of its sensitive axis, the weight moves. A dial connected to the weight shows the acceleration on a scale. This is usually marked in units of feet per second per second (ft/s²), or feet per second squared.

Angular accelerometers

The angular accelerometer works in much the same way. But it is designed to measure the acceleration of a turning body, such as the flywheel of an engine. In this type of instrument, the weight is in the form of a disc. The acceleration of the turning body makes the disc turn and tighten a spiral spring. The amount by which the disc turns indicates the angular acceleration of the body. This is measured in the same units as linear acceleration. The measurement varies according to the distance from the center of rotation.

See also: INERTIAL GUIDANCE SYSTEMS

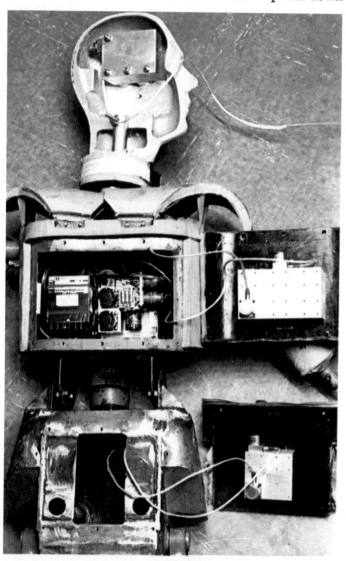

Left: This dummy is used in an automobile accident laboratory. The steel boxes in the head, chest and abdomen are accelerometers.

Below: The gyroscopes in this accelerometer sense any change of direction and feed information to a computer which calculates the new position.

Acids

Acids play an important part in all our lives. We take in dilute citric acid, ascorbic acid and acetic acid in our food. But in industry, the most important acids are strong ones such as sulfuric acid. Millions of tons of this important acid are made every year.

Acids are a group of chemicals, usually in liquid form, that can be recognized by their sour taste and their ability to react with other substances. Together with other chemicals, called BASES and SALTS, they form three of the most important kinds of chemical compounds. A base is the opposite of an acid and when mixed together they neutralize one another. Bases that dissolve in water are called alkalis. When an acid is mixed with a base it forms a salt plus water.

There is one way to tell the difference between an acid and an alkali. If you take a piece of special blue paper called LITMUS PAPER and dip it into an acid, the paper will turn red. If you then dip it into an alkali it will turn blue again. Litmus paper is called an INDICATOR. It is made from lichen plants.

Inorganic acids

There are many different kinds of acids, but they are all divided into two main groups. The first group is the inorganic acids. All inorganic acids contain hydrogen.

The most important inorganic acids are sulfuric acid, hydrochloric acid and nitric acid. They are used in the production of plastics, textiles, explosives, metals, dyes, fertilizers and many other things. The liquid in automobile batteries is dilute sulfuric acid.

Hydrochloric acid is a strong acid, but we have small quantities of it in our stomachs to help us digest our food. If we have too much of it we suffer from "acid stomach." To stop this complaint we take milk of magnesia, or magnesium hydroxide, which is a base that will neutralize the acid.

The organic acids

The organic acids contain carbon atoms. They are not as strong as inorganic acids. Acetic acid is best known in the form of vinegar. It is used in making drugs and chemicals. Lactic acid is formed when milk goes sour. It is used in making cheese. Ascorbic acid is the chemical name for vitamin C. It is found in lemons, limes, oranges, tomatoes and green vegetables. People who do not have any ascorbic acid suffer from the disease scurvy. We use tartaric acid in baking powder.

Amino acids are a group of acids that contain nitrogen. They play an important part in the structure of proteins. We must eat foods containing amino acids to keep ourselves healthy.

See also: ALKALIS, AMINO ACIDS, BATTERY, CHEMISTRY, EXPLOSIVES, PROTEINS

Did you know?

Acid has played an important part in many famous murder cases. In one instance, John George Haigh tried to get rid of a wealthy widow by putting her into a bath full of pure sulfuric acid. This would have worked very well except that her brand new acrylic dentures survived the acid. The teeth were later identified by her dentist and John George Haigh was convicted of murder.

Industry uses huge amounts of sulfuric acid which is made from sulfur in plants like this. This plant uses up about 1500 tons of sulfur a day. The pipes are made of stainless steel so that they will not corrode.

Adhesives

More and more adhesives are being used in industry as well as in the home. Chemists have made new glues that can stick together almost all the parts of an automobile. Superglues can even be sprayed on body wounds to hold skin together and prevent loss of blood.

An adhesive is a substance which bonds (sticks) things together by surface attachment. Glues, pastes and gums are all adhesives.

At one time it was thought that an adhesive worked because it pressed into the pores or cavities of the pieces being stuck together, and when the adhesive hardened into a solid it locked the pieces together. It is now thought that this plays some part in the strength of the join, but is not its main cause.

Adhesion is now thought to be due to chemical forces of the kind that hold the atoms and molecules of materials themselves together. It is known that good adhesion needs the wetting of the two pieces with the adhesive, so that the tiny irregularities of the two surfaces are filled. Even the smoothest surfaces are full of "mountains and valleys" if looked at through a powerful microscope.

Adhesive joints

With most kinds of adhesive, the strength of the joint between the adhesive and the substance it is stuck to is stronger than the adhesive itself. For this reason, it is important to keep the film of adhesive as thin as possible. The surfaces to be stuck together must fit together exactly. They should also have a large enough area in contact to make them stick properly.

More and more joints in industry are being bonded together instead of being bolted or welded. These include metal joints in the automobile and aircraft industries. Back in 1955, the Dutch company Fokker first realized that they could design an aircraft to be stuck together rather than welded or bolted. The F27 Friendship was the result; an aircraft which over many years did not have a single case of adhesive joint failure.

Kinds of adhesives

There are several kinds of natural adhesives, made from animals and vegetables. For many years glue has been made by boiling bones. It is bought in solid form, heated to melt it, and hardens again when it cools.

Natural starches and gums come from various plants. They are used to make light adhesives that dissolve in water. Wallpaper paste and office paste and gum are this type of adhesive. The gum on stamps and envelopes is gum arabic. This gum is made from the sap of an acacia tree that grows in Africa.

Natural rubber, dissolved in chemicals to make it

"runny," and called rubber cement, is used for sticking rubber and leather, and for sticking paper to paper. It can easily be removed without leaving a mark.

Synthetic adhesives

There are many kinds of adhesive that are not animal or vegetable—the SYNTHETIC adhesives. Most of these adhesives are very strong. There are two types: thermosetting and thermoplastic. Thermosetting adhesives get hard when heated, thermoplastic adhesives melt when heated.

Below: Smoothing down a joint between the upper and lower halves of a glass fiber car body. The joint was made with an epoxy resin adhesive.

Bottom: An arched wooden bridge which was stuck together with adhesive.

Among the thermoplastic adhesives are the vinyl resins. These all-purpose adhesives stick well to glass and metal. It is this type of adhesive that is used to stick together thin layers of glass that make laminated safety glass for automobile windshields.

Cellulose adhesives consist of chemicals made from plant CELLULOSE. They are quick-drying and waterproof. Most clear household adhesives, including modeling glue, are of this type.

Synthetic rubber (a thermosetting adhesive) is dissolved in various chemicals to make many types of adhesive. These include the contact adhesives which stick firmly together as soon as contact is made between the surfaces. These adhesives are used in automobile manufacture for attaching interior trim panels.

The thermosetting adhesives also include the epoxy resins. They are usually supplied in two parts which have to be mixed together before use. One of the parts is the "hardener." Epoxy resins are the strongest of all adhesives. In one experiment a 10-ton truck was lifted off the ground. It was stuck by epoxy resin to a metal disc only 2 inches (5 centimeters) across.

See also: ATOMS AND MOLECULES, MICROSCOPE, RUBBER, WELDING

Left: The arched concrete beams of the Olympic Stadium and Velodrome in Montreal were built from pieces weighing up to 65 tons each. These pieces were stuck together with epoxy resin adhesives. Special fast-hardening kinds of adhesive were developed so that the joints could be made during the winter, when temperatures were as low as 0°F (−18°C).

Below: How an adhesive works. When it is first applied, the adhesive is liquid (red balls in figure 1). The tiny molecules in the adhesive begin to join together (2). Chains of molecules begin to form (3). These chains go on growing until the adhesive has set hard (4). Well-made adhesive joints can be at least as strong as the rest of the materials joined together.

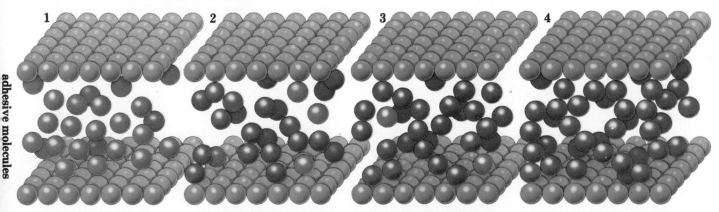

adhesive molecules

molecules of materials being joined together

Aerial Photography

Cameras in modern high-flying airplanes can photograph 20,000 square miles (51,000 square kilometers) in one shot. The quality of the photographs taken is amazing. From a height of 10 miles (16 kilometers) cameras can pick out a detail as small as a golfball.

Aerial photography has many uses in making maps, spying on enemy territory, surveying, prospecting for minerals and archaeology. Photographs taken from satellites cover vast areas and help to improve weather forecasts.

Early history
The French took the earliest aerial photograph, as far as we know. It happened in 1856, less than 20 years after the first proper photographs on earth, and was taken from a balloon.

France continued to lead the world in aerial photography and the French were among the first flyers, too. After the Franco-Prussian War of 1870, they made a survey of the country close to their border with Germany. At first they used balloons, but later they took their cameras into the air in some of the first airplanes. During the 1914—1918 War with Germany, they were able to send planes to rephotograph places occupied by the Germans. By comparing the new photographs with the earlier prewar ones they could

Below: The photograph of San Francisco was taken from a height of 10 miles (16 km) on infrared film. In most infrared film, red prints as green, green as blue and infrared light as red.

easily spot the new buildings put up by the Germans.

But the first aerial photograph to be used for reconnaissance (military survey) in wartime was taken for the Union army by a photographer in a balloon during the American Civil War. This photograph was taken of the Confederate army at Richmond, Virginia, in 1862.

First designs

All the early aerial photographs were taken with the bellows cameras used for ordinary photography. But they were not very satisfactory, since they had to be held over the side of the airplane, where they were blown about by the wind. So the British designed a camera that took photographs through a hole cut in the floor of the airplane, the first camera to be specially created for the job.

The British army reconnaissance unit, under the pioneer pilot J. T. C. Moore-Brabazon (later Lord Brabazon), was the first to use stereo photography so as to see the ground in three dimensions. At the end of World War I aerial reconnaissance was done with complex cameras with large lenses to show up as much as possible of the features on the ground.

Between the wars

After the war the lessons learned in aerial reconnaissance were put to good use in peacetime, mainly for map making.

But when Germany was clearly preparing for another war, the British aerial photographer Sidney Cotton was asked to fly over Germany and photograph all the military bases he could without being caught. In a fast airplane specially fitted out with three hidden cameras, he flew around Germany. He even took important German officers up with him for pleasure trips while he took pictures of their bases.

One of the problems of early aerial photography was that the lens misted over in the cold air, and the mechanism sometimes even froze solid. Cotton's solution was to have warm air blowing over the cameras. Later, during World War II, electric heaters, like tiny electric fires, were used.

World War II

In 1939, when World War II began, the Spitfire was one of the fastest planes in the world. Cotton installed two cameras in the wings and took it over the German frontier area at 33,000 feet (10,000 meters) photographing as he went. Later other fast planes were used in the same way, including the famous Mosquito.

Modern aerial photography

Since World War II there have been many advances in aerial photography. To make a map from aerial photographs, a plane fitted with a camera pointing down-

Top: This aircraft "reconnaissance pod" holds radar and an infrared scanner as well as an ordinary camera. The huge cameras of earlier years are no longer needed. Improved film and lenses give much better detail.

Center and bottom: Two pictures show the German rocket research station at Peenemunde before and after it was bombed in 1943. Research and tests were carried out here on the V-1 flying bomb and the V-2 rocket.

ward sweeps the area to be mapped. Photographs are taken in a series of overlapping steps. The camera is set off automatically every few seconds so that there is an overlap between one picture and the next. This overlap

Above: An infrared photograph can show the difference between areas of healthy (red) and diseased (blue) vegetation. It also shows up the depth of water—light and dark blue areas.

is necessary for STEREOSCOPIC viewing. The airplane then turns and flies back to photograph another strip. There is also an overlap between strips.

The strips of photographs can be matched together to make an air mosaic map. However, the photographs do not give a true picture because of the tilt of the plane or variations in its height. Mountains and valleys appear out of position and proportion in the photographs because they are all at different distances from the camera. But accurate maps can be made if the exact position and height of some points have been fixed by a ground plan. These points can be compared with the information given by the aerial photographs and the whole map adjusted.

Infrared photography

Aerial photographs are often taken by INFRARED light—the invisible rays given off by heating objects. Using a special film, the camera can record these rays just as though they were light instead of heat. Infrared light can penetrate haze and mist, and so infrared aerial photographs are often much clearer than ordinary photographs. Pictures can also be taken in complete darkness.

Different kinds of plants (for example, broad-leaved trees, like oaks, and pine trees) give off different amounts of heat. So an infrared aerial photograph of a forest can show up the areas of pine. Lake pollution from a factory can be seen by the warmer water coming from the factory's outlet.

See also: ARCHAEOLOGICAL TECHNIQUES, CAMERA, MAP MAKING, SATELLITES, WEATHER FORECASTING

Aerodynamics

When you walk against a strong wind you become very aware that air can hold you back. Aerodynamics is the study of the way in which air moves around objects. Scientists use aerodynamics chiefly when designing airplanes, but the same laws apply to automobiles, ships, bridges and skyscrapers.

The main purpose of aerodynamics is the design of shapes that will offer the least resistance to the flow of air. This is called streamlining. The air offers great resistance to any object moving faster than about 20 mph (30 km/h), but the air resistance at any speed depends on the shape of that object.

In the flight of airplanes, the resistance of air is used to give the "lift" that takes the plane up. If there were no air, ordinary aircraft could not take off. However, this does not apply to spaceships. The downward thrust of their rocket motors can safely lift them off the moon, where there is no air at all. They do not rely on the airfoil shape of wings to lift them from the ground.

The airfoil shape

The upper surface of an aircraft wing is curved, and the bottom surface is almost flat. This is an airfoil shape. The curved top allows the air to move faster across the top than across the bottom of the wing. Because the pressure of any gas such as air gets less the faster it goes, the air pressure on top of the wing is less than the pressure beneath it. So the wing is lifted up as the air flows across it.

Engineers are always looking for ways to increase the lift of airplanes and at the same time reduce the resistance (drag) of the air. This is very important to the airlines because nearly half of their costs are spent on buying fuel to feed their thirsty jets. Therefore, the better the streamlining of an airplane, the less fuel it will use.

Wind tunnels

To study the aerodynamics of objects, scientists make great use of wind tunnels. In a wind tunnel, an even flow of air at a controlled speed is blown along by powerful fans.

Scale models of airplanes, automobiles or anything else being studied are hung in the airstream. They are connected to instruments which measure the forces on different parts of them. Complicated math is needed to work out the results of wind tunnel tests. Special photographs are also used.

Below: Colored smoke is often used to study the aerodynamic lines of new car designs.

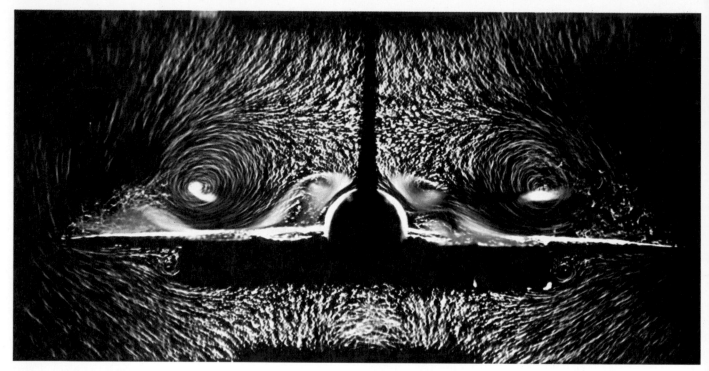

Faster than sound

When an airplane moves at subsonic speed—less than the speed of sound—the air flow builds up pressure ahead of the plane. This pressure creates a wave pattern in the air ahead. This warning wave moves at the speed of sound—about 760 mph (1220 km/h). On receiving the warning, the air ahead of the plane is forced into a pattern that makes room for the plane.

But if the airplane is traveling at supersonic speed—faster than the speed of sound—things are quite different. The air ahead of the plane has no time to prepare for the oncoming wing, and the wing strikes the air ahead with a sudden shock. This causes the shock wave which is heard as a loud bang by people on the ground. Sometimes these shock waves are powerful enough to break windows in houses which are under the airplane's flight path.

Above: Wind tunnel tests can show the flow of air around a model of the airplane.

The best shapes

The best shape for an object moving through air at a speed slower than the speed of sound is that of a falling drop of water. This drop shape, rounded at the front and pointed at the tail, gives less air drag than any other.

But this drop-of-water shape does not work with objects traveling faster than the speed of sound. Supersonic airplanes have sharply-pointed noses. This is because the nose of these planes has continually to pierce a wall of undisturbed air.

See also: AIR, AIRFOIL, AIRPLANES, SUPERSONIC FLIGHT

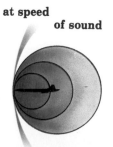

slower than
speed of sound

waves at
speed of sound

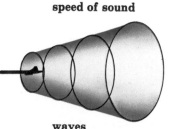

at speed
of sound

waves form shock wave

faster than
speed of sound

waves
spread out behind jet

boom
zone

Aerosol Spray Can

The first patent for an aerosol spray can was taken out in the U.S. in 1941. Products available in spray cans now include paints, cosmetics, insecticides, whipped cream and many household articles.

The design of an aerosol spray can is very simple. At the top of the aerosol can is a plastic valve to control the spray. From the bottom of this valve, a flexible dip tube runs down to the bottom of the can. The can is filled with the product to be sprayed and the propellant, a compressed gas which mixes with the product. The gas is partly liquefied by the pressure in the can, but there is still a layer of gas above the liquid. As the can is emptied, more of the liquefied gas turns into VAPOR to fill the space.

The plastic valve is held shut by the pressure in the can and by a coil spring. When the button is pressed it forces the valve down, uncovering a small hole. The product is forced up the dip tube by the pressure in the can. The propellant and the product leave the nozzle together and the propellant evaporates as soon as it reaches the air, breaking the product into tiny droplets. The same idea, used with a thicker liquid and a wider nozzle, results in foam.

Aerosol cans are filled on the production line by inserting the product, putting the lid and valve on the can and then forcing the propellant in backwards through the valve.

Aerosol hazards
The popularity of the aerosol spray can created a potential world health hazard. Some of the propellants used contained fluorocarbons which threatened to destroy the ozone layer in the ATMOSPHERE. This is the layer which filters out the bulk of the harmful ultraviolet radiation from the sun. There is now strict federal control on the choice of aerosol propellants.

See also: AIR, PRESSURE

Below: A modern aerosol spray can. Gas pressure forces liquid down the can and up the dip tube to the nozzle when the pushbutton valve is opened.

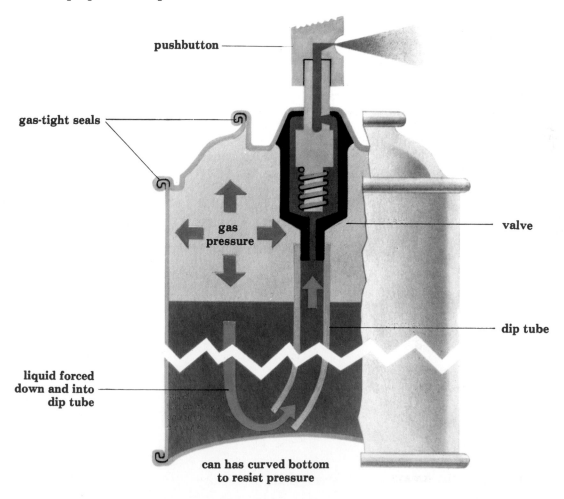

pushbutton

gas-tight seals

gas pressure

liquid forced down and into dip tube

can has curved bottom to resist pressure

valve

dip tube

Air

The air is a mixture of gases without which we could not live. Besides allowing us to breathe, the air also protects us during the day from harmful radiation from the sun. Also, without the heat retained by the air, even places on the Equator would freeze at night.

Air pressure
Since clean air is invisible, tasteless and odorless, we tend to forget that it is there at all. And yet the ATMOSPHERE is made up of around 5,000 million million tons of air. This presses down on the earth's surface. At sea level, the air pressure is equal to about 15 pounds per square inch. So, on our head and shoulders, there is a total pressure of about one ton! Fortunately, the pressure inside our bodies is the same as the pressure outside. This balance of pressures ensures that we are not crushed by the atmosphere.

The effect of air pressure can be shown by gradually pumping out the air from a closed tin can. As the air pressure inside decreases, the air pressure outside crushes the can. Details of this project can be found in Volume 25.

As your height above sea level increases, the air pressure decreases. This is because the higher you go, the less air there is above you. At an altitude (height) of 11 miles (18 kilometers), the air pressure is about one-tenth of that at sea level. And, at 31 miles (50 kilometers), it is only one-thousandth of the sea level pressure.

Besides altitude, the temperature and other factors affect the air pressure at any location. A reading of the air pressure can be used to help forecast the weather. A high-pressure area, for example, is usually associated with fair weather. Weather forecasters measure the air pressure using instruments called barometers.

Layers of the atmosphere
About 80 percent of the air is concentrated in the lowest layer of the atmosphere—the troposphere. Above this are the stratosphere, mesosphere and thermosphere. The air pressure at the bottom of the thermosphere is extremely small. And it decreases with altitude until the thermosphere fades into space.

The region above the stratosphere and extending to about 250 miles (400 kilometers) is often called the ionosphere. It contains charged particles called ions. The outermost zone, above 250 miles, is sometimes referred to as the exosphere.

What is air?
Dry air consists mainly of three gases: nitrogen (78.09 percent), oxygen (20.95 percent) and argon (0.93 percent). The other 0.03 percent consists mainly of the gases carbon dioxide, helium, hydrogen, krypton, methane, neon, ozone and xenon. The air in the lowest

Below left: A cloud of smog hangs over the city of Santiago in Chile. Smog is caused by dirt and gases polluting the air.

Below right: Mountaineers often wear oxygen masks when climbing high peaks. The mountain air is thin, with little oxygen.

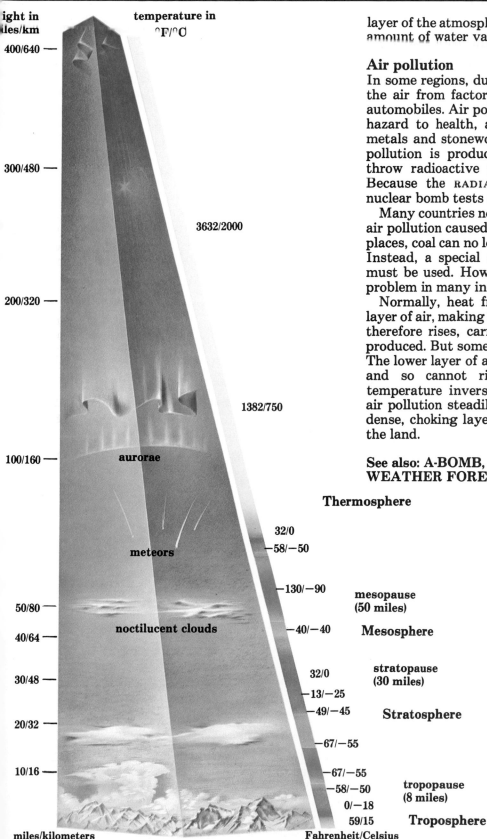

height in
miles/km

400/640 —

300/480 —

200/320 —

100/160 —

50/80 —
40/64 —

30/48 —

20/32 —

10/16 —

miles/kilometers

temperature in
°F/°C

3632/2000

1382/750

aurorae

meteors

noctilucent clouds

32/0
—58/—50

—130/—90

—40/—40

32/0

—13/—25
—49/—45

—67/—55

—67/—55
—58/—50
0/—18
59/15

Fahrenheit/Celsius

Thermosphere

mesopause
(50 miles)

Mesosphere

stratopause
(30 miles)

Stratosphere

tropopause
(8 miles)

Troposphere

layer of the atmosphere also contains water VAPOR. The amount of water vapor is quite small.

Air pollution

In some regions, dust, smoke and harmful gases enter the air from factories, or from the exhaust pipes of automobiles. Air pollution of this kind can be a serious hazard to health, and it may also damage exposed metals and stonework. The most harmful form of air pollution is produced by nuclear explosions. These throw radioactive particles and gases into the air. Because the RADIATION is so harmful to humans, nuclear bomb tests are carried out in remote regions.

Many countries now have laws aimed at reducing the air pollution caused by factories and vehicles. In some places, coal can no longer be used as a fuel in the home. Instead, a special smokeless fuel derived from coal must be used. However, air pollution is still a major problem in many industrial countries.

Normally, heat from the ground warms the lower layer of air, making it expand and become less dense. It therefore rises, carrying away any pollution as it is produced. But sometimes, the ground becomes chilled. The lower layer of air then becomes cooler and denser, and so cannot rise. This condition is called a temperature inversion. When it occurs, the level of air pollution steadily builds up. In the worst cases, a dense, choking layer of smog (smoky fog) hangs over the land.

See also: A-BOMB, BAROMETERS, WEATHER FORECASTING

The diagram shows the layers of the atmosphere, from sea level to the fringes of space. Of particular interest is the way that the temperature changes. At first, it falls steadily with height above sea level. It reaches a minimum of around −67°F (−55°C) at the top of the troposphere. This region is called the tropopause. The temperature then rises to about 32°F (0°C), falls to −130°F (−90°C), then rises steeply. Although temperatures are extremely high in the upper thermosphere, it is not at all like a furnace. This is because there are so few gas particles present at this great height.

23

Air Conditioning

Air conditioning is a means of controlling the climate in a building. It is used to provide comfortable temperatures in theaters, stores, offices and homes. The air is "conditioned"—purified, cooled or heated, and made more or less moist, as required.

Air conditioning systems

The smallest type of air conditioning system consists of a wall-mounted unit serving just the room in which it is located. In large systems, the conditioned air is circulated around the whole building through ducts. These may consist of large metal tubes. In modern buildings, the structure itself often provides the ducts for circulating the air.

Three main types of air conditioning system are used in large buildings: the all-air, air-water and all-water. In the all-air system, a central conditioning plant supplies all the air at a fixed temperature. Smaller units around the building provide the final temperature control. An

alternative is to have two ducts, one carrying cool air and the other carrying warm air. In any area, the required temperature is obtained simply by letting in a suitable mixture of cool and warm air.

In another kind of all-air system, the temperature is regulated by controlling the amount of air supplied instead of its temperature. This is known as a variable-volume system. If a building is to be cooled, then cold air must be provided. But, with this system, its temperature is not critical.

In the air-water system, the central plant provides

Below: A diagram of a typical all-air system that might be used for a large building. For simplicity, the building is represented here by just one room. Air leaves the room through an exhaust duct (bottom left). After being mixed with fresh air from outside, it is passed through two filters, past cooling and heating tubes, and then through an odor filter. After being humidified, a fan returns the air to the room via a silencer.

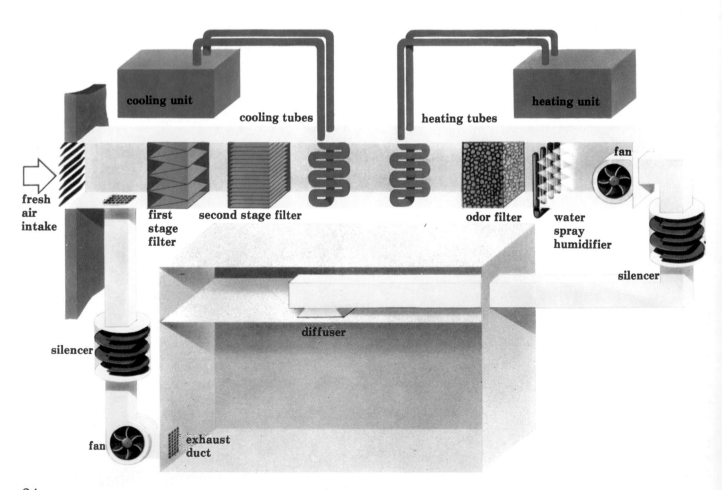

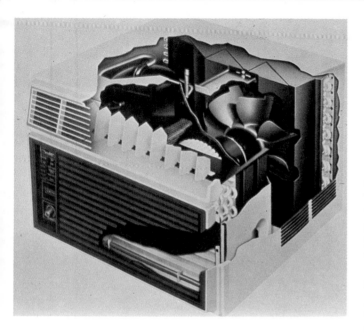

only the fresh air needed for ventilation. For temperature control, each room has its own heating and cooling unit. This uses circulating water kept at a comfortable temperature.

In the all-water system, only the heating or cooling water is supplied by the central plant. Fresh air is brought in through ventilators provided in each room.

The air-water and all-water systems can use small ducts. They are economical to operate and run quietly. The all-air system requires much larger ducts. But it provides a more effective service, with all the air in the building constantly being conditioned.

Air conditioning techniques

In a large, all-air system, fresh air from outside is first drawn in through a duct. It is then mixed with recycled air from the building, for only a certain amount of fresh air is required. This provides the oxygen that we use up when we breathe. The mixed air passes through a filter section, which is usually in two stages.

The first stage often uses a substance like absorbent cotton. When the air passes through the fibers, any large dust particles get left behind.

The second stage filter removes fine particles, such as cigarette smoke. This is usually done by passing the air through a series of metal plates carrying a high electrical charge. These plates attract light objects. So, as the air passes through, the fine particles are left clinging to the plates.

Assuming that the air is to be supplied at a fixed temperature, it then passes two sets of tubes. The first set carries hot water or steam. Chilled water, or a special refrigerant (cooling) fluid passes through the

other tubes. An instrument in the building measures the air temperature. If this is too high, the cooling tubes are automatically brought into operation. If the air temperature is too low, the heating tubes are used instead. In this way, the circulated air is always kept at the same temperature.

Odor filter

After undergoing temperature control, the air passes through an odor filter. This is made from a substance called activated carbon. It can absorb (soak up) large numbers of odor molecules from the air. From time to time, it has to be taken out and reactivated by heating. The heat drives off the absorbed material, restoring the filter to its original condition, ready to be used again.

Finally, moisture is added to the air to produce the desired HUMIDITY. Either steam is injected into the air, or a spray of fine water droplets is used. A device called a hygrometer measures the humidity in the building. This instrument automatically controls the amount of moisture added to the air, to make sure it is kept at a suitable level. If there is too much moisture, the air is usually cooled and then reheated at the temperature control stage. In the cooling process, the moisture CONDENSES to form water drops on the cold tubes.

Sound absorber

The conditioned air is normally moved around the system by a CENTRIFUGAL fan. Air taken in near the center of the fan is forced outward by its large, curved blades. To prevent noise from the fan reaching the main part of the building, the air is passed through a silencer. This contains material that absorbs most of the sound energy from the air stream. The air then flows along ducts, and enters the rooms through diffusers. These take various forms, such as long slots or grilles high in the walls.

Ordinary air conditioning systems are often changed to provide special requirements. In operating rooms, for example, the air supply must be germ-free to reduce the risk of infection. In aircraft, the air conditioning system is made mostly of aluminum or light alloy in order to be as lightweight as possible.

See also: ALLOYS, ALUMINUM, HYGROMETER

Air-Cushion Vehicles

If someone had suggested 30 years ago that one day over 400 people and 60 automobiles would go speeding across the water at 80 miles per hour (128 km/h) on a cushion of air, nobody would have believed it. This is now a fast and safe everyday event.

Air-cushion vehicles (ACVs) are propeller-driven machines that speed across water or land on a "cushion" of air blown downward by fans. Because they are not in contact with the sea or land, they have many advantages.

Making waves

Large, modern ACVs (also called hovercraft or ground-effect machines) can skim over waves up to 10 feet (3 meters) high at speeds of 70 knots (the nautical measurement for 80 mph). A large ship cannot travel at this speed because the VISCOSITY of the water holds back the underwater part of the ship.

A ship also makes waves, and these take energy from the ship which has to push the water away. This is why it is much more difficult to walk waist-deep in water than in air or on land. The larger and faster the ship, the greater the amount of energy wasted in powering it through the water.

Since no part of the air-cushion vehicle is underwater, it does not have these problems.

How the air-cushion vehicle works

The idea behind the ACV is very simple. Air is blown down through the middle of the craft by a large motor-driven fan. If this is done with a flat-bottomed boat, the air just escapes round the edges, and the craft is not lifted clear of the water.

The air must be held under the boat somehow to give the "lift." At first the designers tried putting a steel edge around their flat-bottomed boat, rather like a tray fixed upside down to the bottom. They also directed air into the "tray" through jets around the edge which all pointed inward toward the middle of the boat. This helped to enclose the air.

But the greatest improvement came when they put a rubber "skirt" around the outside of the boat's bottom. This held the air in place better than the steel. Also it did not drag in the water, and so there were no problems with viscosity and waves. In fact modern ACVs are so efficient that a craft weighing 100 tons can be lifted one foot on its air cushion using a pressure of less than half a pound per square inch. An ordinary car tire may need 40 or 50 times more pressure.

How the ACV developed

Engineers tried to solve the ACV's problems in the early 1930s, but little was done until World War II.

It was the British engineer, C. S. Cockerell, who designed and built the first ACV that really worked. He used the "tray" idea, but the steel edges were fixed only to the sides of the ship, not to the front and back. First of all he tried hinged flaps to hold the air in. These did not work very well, and so he next tried pumping water in a high-pressure stream instead of the flaps. But still the air escaped too easily, and he finally came up with the idea of pumping jets of air downward all around the outside of the bottom of the craft. This at last proved to be the answer.

Below: The ACV below is a *Voyageur*, developed for use in Canada, where problems such as frozen lakes in winter make it ideal for carrying cargo.

Above: A British Army ACV on duty in the Malayan jungle. This type can seat 18 passengers or carry 2 tons of freight.

Left: A U.S. Navy patrol ACV on a mission in the Mekong Delta.

The first journey

The first ACV in the world, the SR-N1, took to the sea in 1959. It made the 6-mile (9.6-kilometer) voyage from the Isle of Wight, where she was built, to the south coast of England. Later she took only two hours to cross from England to France.

Today descendants of the first hovercraft cross every day between England and France. These modern ACVs are 186 feet (57 meters) long, weigh 305 tons and cruise at more than 70 mph (112 km/h).

But these big passenger craft are dwarfed by the U.S. Navy's Large Surface Effect Ship (LSES) built by Bell Aerospace. This giant weighs 3000 tons and looks like a small aircraft carrier. It carries vertical take-off airplanes and can, of course, travel much faster than an ordinary ship.

Uses of the ACVs

The ACV can move from land to sea and back again with ease. All it needs is a gently sloping beach. No expensive harbor facilities are required.

The advantages are especially useful for military and naval purposes. At sea, the ACV can fire torpedoes, but it cannot be torpedoed itself. Any torpedo just goes underneath the hovering craft.

The ACV on land

There are many uses for the air-cushion vehicle on dry land—from the hovering lawn mower to large air-cushion transporters that carry heavy loads around factories. The American ACT 375 is a craft designed to carry a 375-ton PAYLOAD across the Arctic wastes.

But there are disadvantages

Although an ACV can travel faster and use less power than a ship of the same size, it always uses the same amount of power to lift itself from the water, no matter how slowly it goes. So the ACV is cheap to run only when it is traveling at speed.

There is also a limit to the size of the waves that an air-cushion vehicle can cope with. At the moment, waves of about 10 feet (3 meters) are the limit for these craft.

ACVs are also rather difficult to steer. This is because there is so little FRICTION between the craft and the surface. When an ACV is put into a tight turn it tends to slide sideways. Therefore, ACVs have rather complicated steering methods. The SR-N4, for example, has three steering devices. It has rudders like an airplane at the tail and four propellers which can be swiveled on pylons so that the craft can be moved sideways if necessary. The propellers can be made to go faster on one side of the craft than on the other. In addition, the whole ACV can be made to tilt inward when doing a turn. This is done by adjusting the lifting air jets.

A further disadvantage for passengers is the high noise level from the propellers and the lifting fans. However, ACVs are being increasingly used on medium-distance ferry routes.

See also: HYDROFOIL, LAWN MOWER, PROPELLERS

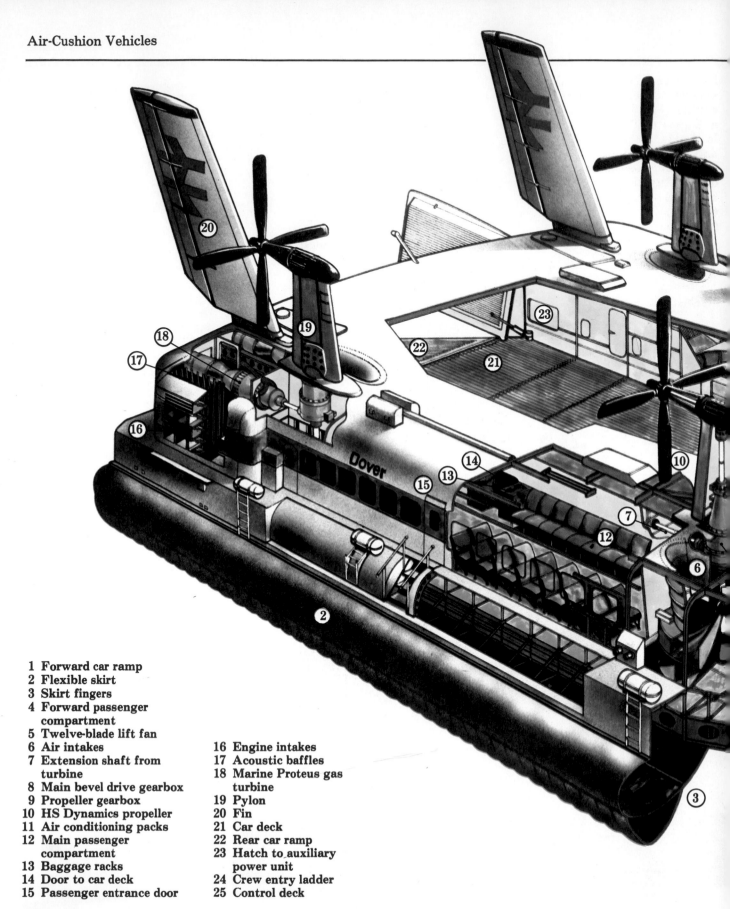

1 Forward car ramp
2 Flexible skirt
3 Skirt fingers
4 Forward passenger
   compartment
5 Twelve-blade lift fan
6 Air intakes
7 Extension shaft from
   turbine
8 Main bevel drive gearbox
9 Propeller gearbox
10 HS Dynamics propeller
11 Air conditioning packs
12 Main passenger
   compartment
13 Baggage racks
14 Door to car deck
15 Passenger entrance door

16 Engine intakes
17 Acoustic baffles
18 Marine Proteus gas
   turbine
19 Pylon
20 Fin
21 Car deck
22 Rear car ramp
23 Hatch to auxiliary
   power unit
24 Crew entry ladder
25 Control deck

Below: The SR-N4 air-cushion vehicle. It has four gas turbine engines, each driving one lift fan and one propeller. Air is sucked in through vents in the top deck and forced into a large space just under the passenger and car decks. From here it goes into the tube-like skirt around the edge of the craft and is forced inward to form a cushion of air.

air enters intake

lift fan

flexible skirt

some air escapes

inside air chamber

Above: This diagram shows how the air is forced down and inward to form a cushion between the craft and the surface. The flexible rubber skirt helps to stop the air escaping too quickly.

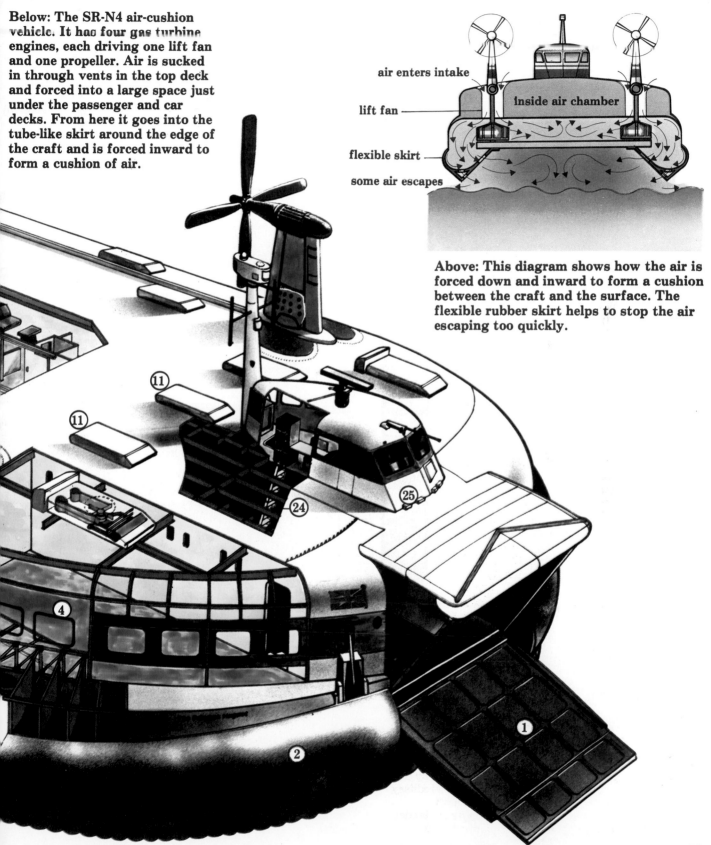

Airfoil

An airfoil is a body shaped so that it produces a force as it moves through the air. Aircraft wings are airfoils that produce a lifting force to support the plane. Racing cars have airfoils with a downward force that helps hold them on the road.

The upper side of an aircraft wing seen in cross section is curved, and the lower side mostly flat. This difference in CURVATURE is found in all airfoils, and is the reason for the forces they produce. As the wing moves through the air, the front edge splits the air it meets into two streams. One stream passes over the wing, and the other passes underneath. The two airstreams rejoin behind the rear edge of the wing.

Because the upper surface of the wing is more curved, the upper airstream has farther to travel than the lower airstream. So it follows that the upper airstream has to move over the surface faster than the lower airstream in order to reach the rear edge of the wing at the same time. This difference in speed gives rise to a difference in air pressure on the two surfaces of the wing.

Different pressures

Bernoulli's principle, named after the Swiss scientist Daniel Bernoulli, states that the faster a gas, such as air, moves, the lower its pressure. The faster airflow over the upper surface, therefore, produces a smaller pressure on the wing than does the airflow underneath. The effect of these unequal pressures is an upward force under the wing. In this way, the forward movement of an aircraft produces forces that lift it in the air.

Bernoulli's principle applies to liquids too, so airfoil shaped devices also work in water. Known as hydrofoils, these can be used to lift the hull of a boat out of the water. This reduces the backward drag of the water, allowing the boat to attain a higher speed than normal.

Racing cars are sometimes fitted with an airfoil at the front and back. The airfoils used on cars are often

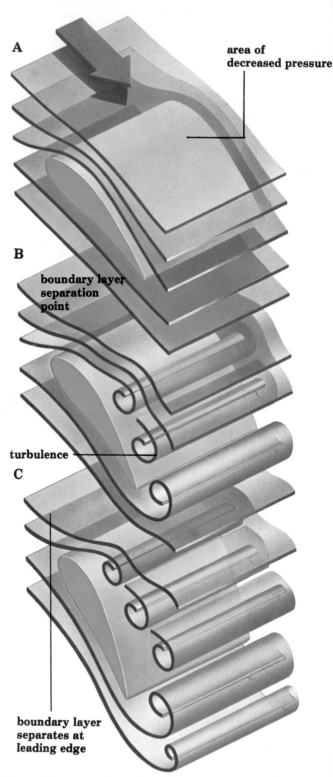

area of decreased pressure

boundary layer separation point

turbulence

boundary layer separates at leading edge

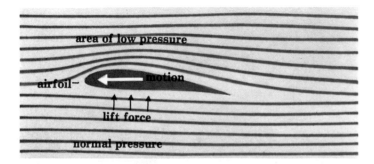

Above: This diagram shows how air rushes faster over the top of the airfoil shape than below it. This makes a difference in pressure which pushes the wing up and lifts the plane.

Above: At normal speeds, there is little turbulence (A). At lower speeds (B and C), the air layer on the wing top separates, eventually causing the plane to stall.

described as being upside down, because they have curved lower surfaces and flat upper surfaces. As a result, they work in the opposite way to aircraft wings. They create downward force when the car moves forward. The faster the car moves, the greater the downward pressure produced. This gives the car the better grip on the road surface it needs when racing at high speed.

Sometimes we may think of an airfoil as being at rest, with the air rushing past it. At other times, it may be easier to understand what is happening by thinking of the airfoil moving through stationary air. But, as long as one of them is moving, the same basic principle applies. Aircraft designers test stationary model aircraft in wind tunnels. They study the air pressure patterns produced on the wings and body. By doing this, they can see how the real aircraft will perform when moving through the air.

Other examples of airfoils include the blades of fans, propellers and helicopter rotors. Although different in appearance to the wings of an airplane, they do have the curved surfaces that cause pressure differences when they move through the air. All types of airfoil need careful design if they are to work efficiently. Modern aircraft wings are designed with the aid of computers.

Airfoil limitations

As long as the flow of air over a wing remains smooth, it produces useful lift. The smooth, continuous airstream required is called a LAMINAR FLOW. The air moves in

Above: The airfoils fitted to this racing car have curved lower surfaces. The downward pressure produced helps hold the car down.

layers, the one nearest to the wing moving more slowly than layers farther away. The same effect can be seen in rivers, where the flow near the banks is slower than in the middle.

The lift produced by a wing can be increased by tilting its front edge so that it is higher than the back edge. This increases the distance that the upper airstream has to travel. So the pressure difference and, hence, the lift are increased too. The angle by which the wing is tilted is called its angle of attack.

Angle of attack

When an ordinary airplane is traveling at a slow speed, its wings must have a relatively large angle of attack. In this way, sufficient lift can still be produced to keep the plane airborne. You may have noticed the nose up attitude of airliners as they come in slowly to land. But the angle of attack cannot be increased indefinitely. For the pressure above the rear edge of the wing eventually becomes so low that the air layer separates from it. The laminar flow then becomes turbulent (irregular) and the plane will stall.

See also: AERODYNAMICS, AIRPLANES, HELICOPTER, HYDROFOIL, RACING CAR

Airplanes

When we talk about airplanes we mean flying machines that are heavier than air. The first real airplane was the Wright brothers' *Flyer* which stayed in the air for 12 seconds. Today's planes can travel faster than the speed of sound for 11 hours nonstop.

To fly, an airplane must lift itself off the ground against the force of the earth's gravity. This lift is produced by air flowing over the aircraft's wings, which have a special shape called an airfoil. The wings are curved at the top and flat at the bottom. Air passing over the top of the wing travels faster because it has farther to go. This means that the air pressure above the wing is less than below it. The wing is therefore sucked upward.

Getting off the ground
An airplane has to reach a certain speed before there is enough lift to get it off the ground. The faster it goes, the more lift there is. If a plane slows down below what is known as "stalling speed," it will fall out of the sky.

The stalling speed is higher with thin wings than with thick wings. This means that jet aircraft with thin wings need higher takeoff and landing speeds.

However, the pilot can change the shape of the wings by using devices called flaps. Part of the front of the wing, and sometimes the back as well, can be hinged downward. This gives more lift at lower speeds.

Thrust and drag
The thrust (force) needed to push an airplane through the air comes either from a propeller or the exhaust from a jet engine. When air is pushed back by a propeller or by a jet engine, its speed increases—because the air coming toward the front of the engine is at a lower speed than the air rushing away behind it. This difference gives forward thrust to the plane.

This thrust is always opposed by drag—the resistance of the air on the aircraft body and wings. To reduce drag, designers build smooth, streamlined bodies and swept-back wings.

Flying the airplane
Once in the air, an aircraft can change its position from normal straight, level flight in three ways: it can roll (tilt sideways), yaw (side to side) and pitch (nose up and down). The diagrams below show these movements.

To fly an airplane, the pilot uses flight controls.

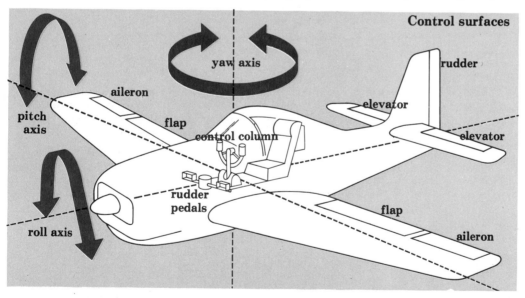

Control surfaces

Left: An airplane has three sets of control surfaces which tilt it in three different ways. The ailerons, which move by turning the control column, make the craft roll. The elevators, worked by moving the control column back or forward, make the craft pitch (point its nose up or down) and thus to climb or dive. The rudder, worked by the foot pedals, makes the craft yaw or swivel.

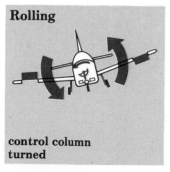

Rolling

control column turned

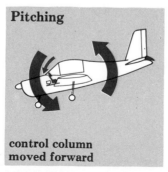

Pitching

control column moved forward

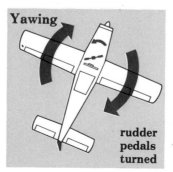

Yawing

rudder pedals turned

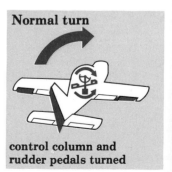

Normal turn

control column and rudder pedals turned

These include the control stick or control wheel, rudder pedals and a throttle. The stick or wheel is pushed forward to lower the plane's nose and backward to raise it. It also moves sideways to bank the plane. The stick is connected by cables to the elevator in the tail unit of the plane. Pushing the stick forward tilts the elevator down at the back. This pushes the whole tail unit up and the nose down. Pulling the stick backward lowers the tail and raises the nose.

Wing control

The control stick is also connected to cables which run

Right, top: Flaps are mounted at the back edge of the wing. Their action is sometimes helped by a front edge "droop." When the flaps are lowered, the wing has more lift at slow speeds. The small airflow through the gap between the flap and the wing smooths out any turbulence caused by the flap.

Right: The wings are angled upwards (called dihedral). When the aircraft tilts, the lower wing gives more lift than the upper wing. This brings the airplane level again.

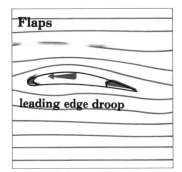
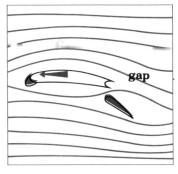

Flaps

leading edge droop

gap

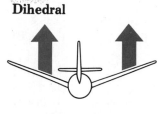
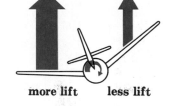

Dihedral

equal amount of lift

more lift   less lift

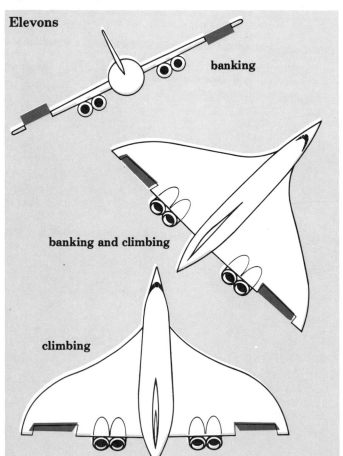

Elevons

banking

banking and climbing

climbing

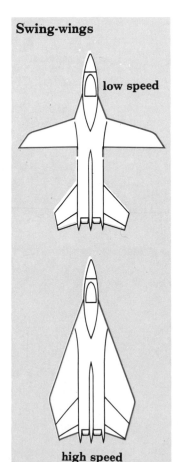

Swing-wings

low speed

high speed

Far left: A delta-winged airplane has no separate tail, so it has no separate ailerons and elevators. It has elevons, single control surfaces that do both jobs. To roll the plane, one elevon is raised and the other lowered. To make it climb, both are raised. For a climbing turn, one elevon is raised and the other remains level.

Near left: Swing-wings are found in some supersonic planes. At low speeds, during takeoff and landing, the wings are straight out for maximum lift. At high speeds they are folded back toward the tail. Control is through elevons on the tail section. There are no ailerons.

along each wing to the ailerons. These are hinged surfaces near the wing tips. When the control stick is pushed to the left, the aileron on the left wing is raised and the aileron on the right wing is lowered. This reduces the flow of air over the left aileron and decreases the lift at that side of the airplane. The left wing is lowered. At the same time, as the aileron on the right wing is lowered its lift is increased. So the airplane banks to the left.

Most aircraft have a wheel instead of a control stick. When the wheel is moved forward or backward, the plane's nose rises or goes down. Turning the wheel to the right or left is the same as moving the control stick in the same direction.

The foot pedals are connected to cables which go to the rudder at the back. When the left pedal is pushed down, the rudder turns to the left and the plane moves

The *Concorde*, **a supersonic airplane, was developed jointly by Britain and France and entered service in 1976. It carries 128 passengers at a cruising speed of 1335 mph (2150 km/h) and has a range of 5145 miles (8280 kilometers). Its long, pointed nose is "dropped" during takeoff and landing (above right) so that the pilot can see the runway.**

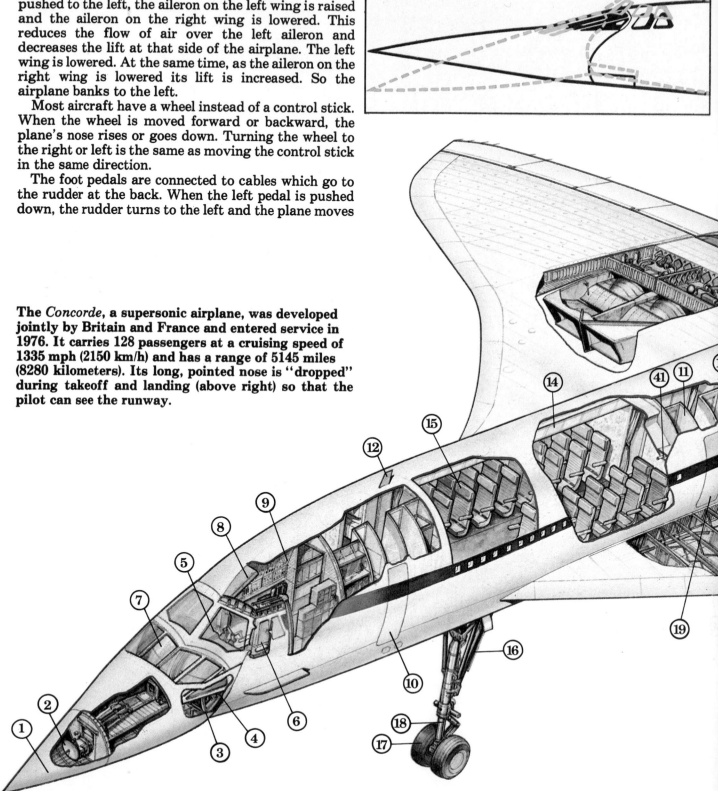

1 Drooping nose
2 Weather radar
3 Droop nose guide rails
4 Retractable visor
5 Instrument panel
6 Pilot's seat
7 Forward pressure bulkhead
8 Switch panel
9 Radio and electronics racks
10 Forward passenger door
11 Toilets
12 VHF antenna
13 Life rafts
14 Overhead baggage racks
15 Four abreast seating
16 Telescopic strut
17 Nose wheel

18 Shock absorber
19 Middle passenger door
20 Servo control unit
21 Fin construction
22 Fin support frames
23 Retractable tail bumper

24 Fuel jettison
25 Rear pressure bulkhead
26 Oxygen bottle storage
27 Rear emergency door
28 Jet exhaust nozzles
29 Accumulator
30 Vent and pressurization
    system
31 RR Bristol/SNECMA
    Olympus 593 turbojets
32 Outer wing fixing
33 Port inner elevon
34 Port outer elevon
35 Static dischargers
36 Fuel tank
37 Wing structure
38 Main undercarriage
39 Main wheel leg
40 Flight deck air duct
41 Cabin air distribution
42 Wheel wells

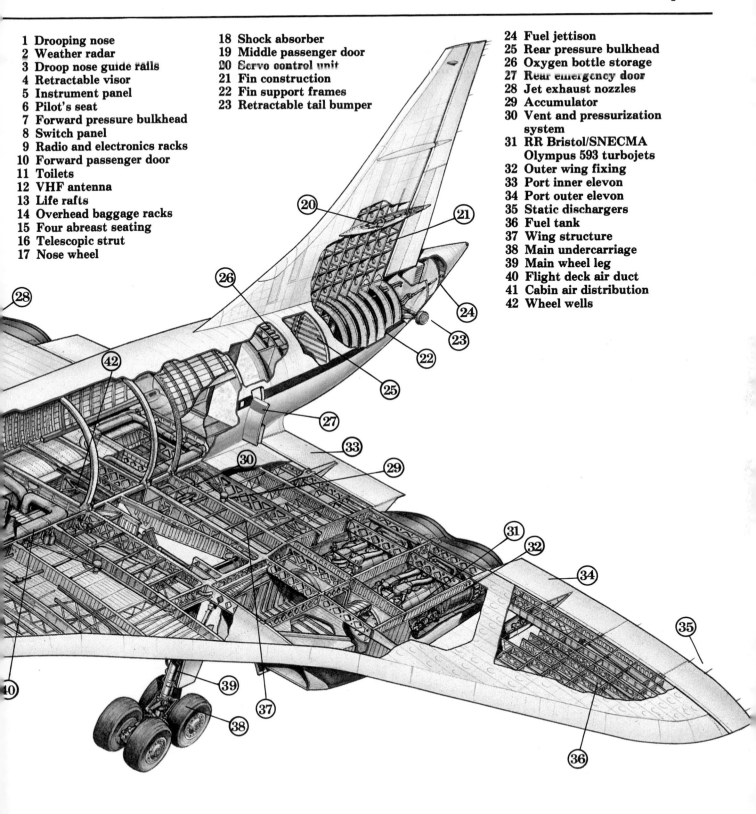

to the left too. By moving the ailerons, the aircraft can be made to bank or roll inwards at the same time as the rudder turns. So the plane tilts as it turns, just as a bicycle does when you turn a corner.

The throttle controls the speed of the engine. In today's high-speed airplanes, the forces on the hinged surfaces such as ailerons and rudder are much too great for the pilot to move them on his own. They are now moved by HYDRAULIC cylinders operated by the pilot through SERVOMECHANISMS. This arrangement is similar to the power steering on an automobile. The

controls of modern aircraft are therefore quite light.

The wings
Nearly all airplane wings are made of metal. They have a skeleton of ribs and spars, covered by a thin layer of light alloy. Most aircraft have wings that are completely supported by the body of the plane (the fuselage). These are called cantilever wings.

In addition to being more curved on top, the front of the wings (the leading edge) are slightly higher than the back (the trailing edge). Most high-speed airplanes

Color code:

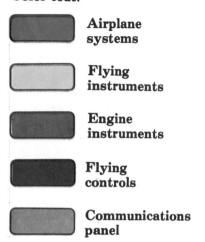

Airplane systems

Flying instruments

Engine instruments

Flying controls

Communications panel

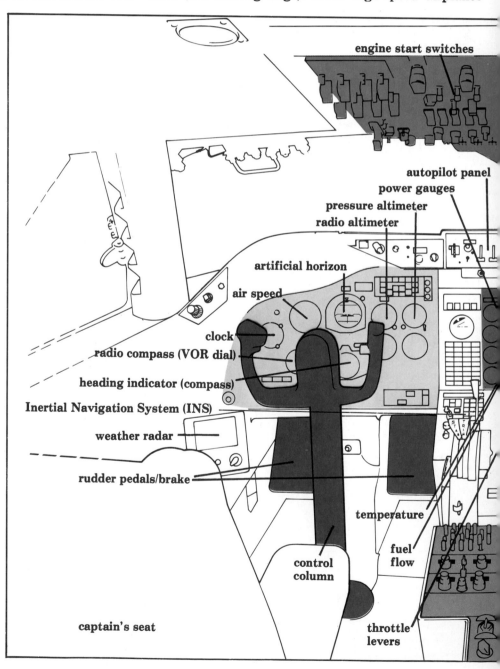

engine start switches

autopilot panel
power gauges
pressure altimeter
radio altimeter

artificial horizon
air speed

clock
radio compass (VOR dial)

heading indicator (compass)

Inertial Navigation System (INS)

weather radar

rudder pedals/brake

temperature

fuel flow

control column

captain's seat

throttle levers

Right: The drawing shows one half of the pilot's control panel; the photograph shows the other half. The captain and the first officer can have the same controls in front of them, so either can fly the airplane. An autopilot system can be switched in when required.

36

have swept-back wings to reduce drag as the wings cut through the air. A delta wing is shaped like a large triangle. This design gives good lift and high speed. However, there is no ideal shape for airplane wings. They have many different shapes, depending on the type of plane and the speed at which it is to fly.

Faster than sound

Supersonic airplanes (airplanes that fly faster than sound) present special problems for those who design them. They have to be a special shape to fly at very high speeds, but they must also fly at low speeds when landing and taking off. To get around this problem, the swing-wing airplane was built. For takeoff and landing, the wings stick out straight to give good lift. But for supersonic flight they are swept back toward the fuselage to form a delta shape.

Vertical takeoff

Another type of plane developed for a special purpose is the vertical takeoff and landing (VTOL) aircraft. Helicopters are really this type of plane because they

Left: An experienced pilot can maneuver his airplane without being able to see anything except his instruments. This is necessary when he is flying at night or in fog. If the pilot cannot see the ground, it is difficult for him to know whether he is on the right course or whether he is going up or down. The instruments in front of him give him all the information he needs about air speed, altitude, rate of climb, and whether the airplane is in level flight. Another group of instruments gives information about engines and other systems—revolution counters, oil pressure, fuel gauge and undercarriage indicator.

Below: Most flight instruments have warning "flags" or lights which appear if anything is wrong or the instrument is not turned on.

Left and below: The air-speed indicator is a most important instrument. It works by air pressure on the airplane. The force of the air on the front of the airplane creates more pressure than there is at the side of the plane. The indicator shows the difference between these two pressures. The faster the plane goes, the greater the difference in pressure. To measure this difference, the airplane has a pitot tube sticking out into the air stream. In the diagram below you can see how the air-speed indicator needle shows the difference between the two air pressures.

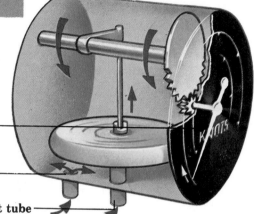

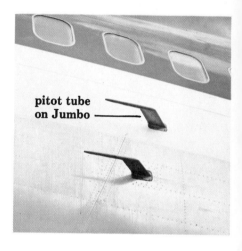

needle shows difference between two pressures, giving air speed

air pressure pipe from side of plane

capsule connected to pitot tube

pitot tube on Jumbo —

are lifted straight up by an overhead rotating blade. VTOL usually means an ordinary plane that has some special system to get it off the ground quickly.

The simplest VTOL planes have fixed jet engines that point downward and lift the aircraft. These jets have nothing to do with pushing the plane forward; other jets have to be added for that purpose.

Another kind of VTOL airplane has jets which can be turned downward for takeoff and brought back to a horizontal position for forward flight. The British Hawker Siddeley *Harrier* is this type of VTOL.

VTOLs have shown themselves very useful in military operations. They can operate without airfields, and in places such as jungles where ordinary airplanes cannot land. VTOLs can also take off and land from small aircraft carriers at sea.

The STOL (short takeoff and landing) airplane is similar to the VTOL, but needs a short runway. These planes are less expensive to make and operate than VTOLs. They have large flaps and other special controls to give quick lift at low speeds.

The fuselage
Every aircraft is made as light as possible. Early planes had wooden frames covered with canvas. Some small craft still have a frame construction covered with glass fiber or aluminum sheet. But faster, high-powered planes have a fuselage in which the outside shell takes a lot of the stress. There is also a framework of light metal alloy. The outer shell is usually a sandwich of two thin layers of alloy glued to a metal "honeycomb" mesh.

The engine
Most airplanes today are powered by jet engines. There are still some that are driven by PISTON ENGINES using gasoline. These engines work in much the same way as automobile engines, but may be air cooled. Propellers do not work well at speeds of more than 450 mph (725 km/h).

Jet engines are much more powerful than piston engines of the same weight. They also use the cheaper fuel, kerosene, but they burn it at an enormous rate —sometimes 1000 gallons an hour or more.

In the cockpit
A dazzling variety of dials and warning lights faces the pilot in the cockpit of a modern airliner. They keep the pilot informed about how the various systems in the aircraft are working and whether he is on course.

The main flight instruments are the altimeter to show the height of the plane, an air-speed indicator and a compass to indicate direction. An automatic pilot keeps the aircraft flying when the pilot leaves the controls.

See also: AIRFOIL, AIR TRAFFIC CONTROL, AVIATION HISTORY, AVIONICS, GYROSCOPE, JET ENGINE, VTOL

Left and below: The artificial horizon tells the pilot whether the plane is flying level or not. It uses a gyroscope, a wheel which is kept spinning at high speed. If you have a toy gyroscope, you will know that it is difficult to tilt it once the wheel is spinning and, in the same way, a toy top stays upright until it starts to slow down. When the airplane banks or climbs, the gyroscope stays level where it is. The aircraft symbol on the dial shows the difference between the level of the gyroscope and the level of the plane. When the symbol and the artificial horizon are parallel, the airplane is flying straight and level.

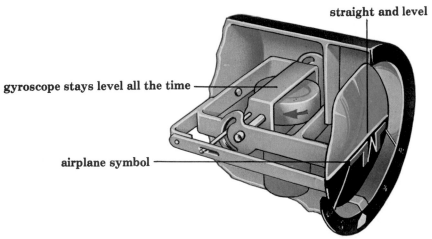

straight and level

gyroscope stays level all the time

airplane symbol

banking to right

DH

F

S

TEST

Below: The instrument below is the pressure altimeter. It tells the pilot how high the airplane is flying. Inside the altimeter, a metal capsule behaves like a balloon. The capsule has air sealed inside it, so the pressure inside it always remains the same. As the plane goes higher, the air pressure around the plane gets less. This reduced air pressure allows the air in the capsule to push the metal of the capsule out. This metal is connected to a lever which turns the pointer arm. A pipe connects the altimeter to the air outside the plane. This is necessary because the air inside the aircraft is kept at a constant pressure.

inside of altimeter is sealed off from cabin air

metal capsule with air sealed inside

needle moves to show height

pipe connects altimeter with the outside air

Airport

Not so long ago, airports were grass fields and a few shacks. Today, airports are vast complexes which form an important part of a country's transport system. They are carefully planned to get the planes up and down safely and move passengers quickly. For safety and noise reasons, they are built well away from city centers.

A big airport needs careful planning. It must have good highways linking it with the city center. There must be plenty of parking space so that passengers can leave their cars within a short walk of the bay in which their airliner is docked. The airlines and the control authorities must also provide check-in counters, passport checkpoints for international flights, passenger lounges and duty-free shops.

In addition to the passengers' requirements, the

airlines themselves need all kinds of help. A big airport may employ 50,000 people. Their jobs include dealing with passengers and their baggage, immigration, servicing and refueling aircraft as well as air traffic control. Nearly as many workers as passengers may go into a big airport each day.

The airplanes
The airliners themselves take up a great deal of space.

Left: An aerial view of John F. Kennedy airport. Nearly all the central space is parking lots. Surrounding these are the airport buildings, then parking and taxying space for aircraft. The runways are on the outside.

Runways 12,000 feet (3.7 kilometers) long and 150 feet (45 meters) wide are needed for today's big jets. Ideally there should be at least two runways, each running in the direction of the prevailing winds (the most usual direction of the wind for that area). There must also be turnoffs and taxiways as close as possible to the terminal.

You can understand the automobile parking problems when you think that each airliner may have 350 seats, and there can be a hundred cars turning up at the airport for each plane. Half a dozen airliners a day may come into each bay.

The airplanes also need a parking area and space in which they can undergo regular maintenance. Since airliners are so expensive to run, they have to be turned around as quickly as possible between flights. Time on the ground has to be kept short. Sometimes the turnaround time may be as short as 20 minutes. In this time, passengers have to get off, the airplane refueled and maintained, cleaned and restocked with food and drink, and the next load of passengers taken on board.

Landing procedures
The airliner approaches an airport to land by ILS (Instrument Landing System). Ground control supplies the approaching aircraft with heading (the direction in

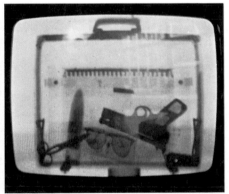

Above: Hand luggage is placed in a special X-ray machine. X-rays pass through most things, but metal objects block their path. A TV camera views the X-ray plate. Metal objects in a case then show up on the screen.

Right: A special "sniffer" hand-held PD5 explosives detector samples the air around the suitcase. Even a tiny trace of the smell of explosives will ring an alarm.

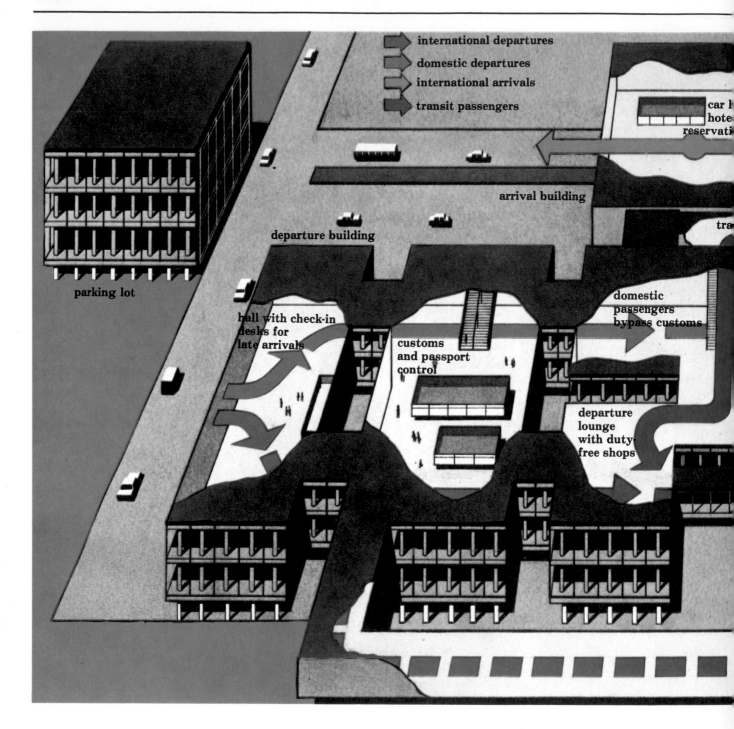

international departures
domestic departures
international arrivals
transit passengers

car h
hote
reservati

arrival building

departure building

tra

parking lot

hall with check-in
desks for
late arrivals

customs
and passport
control

domestic
passengers
bypass customs

departure
lounge
with duty-
free shops

which it should approach) and glidepath information. Airplanes usually begin to line themselves up with the runway at a distance of about 5 to 7 miles (8 to 11 kilometers). They follow guidance beams until they land.

Landing procedures are becoming more and more automatic. Many of the latest planes can approach and land without the pilot touching the controls at all. This is only possible, however, if the airport landing aids are of the most modern type.

Radar
Radar is a valuable partner to ILS. The radar system at an airport usually covers an area of several hundred square miles of airspace around the airport. An incoming airliner is seen as a "blip" on the radar screen.

Above: A simplified diagram of a modern international airport. Routes through the building have to be carefully organized so that passengers going in different directions do not mix. If this happened, it would cause confusion and allow people to avoid ticket and passport checks. Each passenger must be passed through the correct stages, one by one, and in the correct order. The arrangement must also allow for changes if part of the airport has to be closed for repairs. The main need is for plenty of space, but this makes passengers travel great distances when going from one part of the building to another. Escalators and moving sidewalks are helping with this problem in newer airports.

Left: Airplanes cannot stand directly outside the departure terminals and so long pods lead from the terminals to the doors of the airplanes. Cargo trucks load freight and baggage into the holds of the airplanes.

Below, right: A night view of London's Heathrow airport showing lines of aircraft bays connected by passenger jetties.

This blip is used by the air traffic controller to steer the pilot onto the ILS beam.

While waiting to land, a plane circles in what is called a "holding pattern." This is usually a large oval path about 15 miles (24 kilometers) away from the airport. A "stack" is a number of aircraft waiting in the holding pattern, with 1000 feet (300 meters) of height between them. As the bottom plane in the stack begins its approach to the runway, each plane above it is told by traffic control to move down to the next level. Eventually, all the planes are cleared into the airport.

Visual landing aids

Visual landing aids are still very important. The visual approach landing indicator, which is in use day and night, is an "airfield in sight" landing aid. Bars of red and white lights on either side of the runway are set at special angles. The pilot sees only red lights when he is below the correct glidepath, and only white lights when he is too high. When he is on the correct glidepath he sees both red and white lights. These lights are on either side of the part of the runway where the pilot should touch down.

The close approach to the runway is indicated by approach lighting—a white center line crossed by white bars. These bars appear narrower as the runway approaches.

The lights fitted into the runway itself have to be carefully designed to take the weight of a large plane landing. They also have to be level with the ground so that the landing is not bumpy. The powerful lights shine through narrow slits no more than ½ inch (13 millimeters) high.

Keeping the runways clear

Runways have to be kept clear of stones or anything that might cause a plane to suffer a burst tire. A great deal of money, therefore, has to be spent on special runway vacuum cleaners and sweepers. To clear snow, machines with plow-blades, brushes and blowers are used. The amount spent on snow-clearing varies a great deal from place to place, depending on how much snow a particular airfield can expect each year.

Thankfully, the airport's least-used equipment is its fire, crash and rescue vehicles. As aircraft became bigger and bigger, there had to be large increases in the quantities of fire-extinguishing material, such as foam, that might be needed. Modern fire trucks can give a "knockout punch" of large quantities of foam in one minute so that people can get out of the airplane.

A fleet of trucks carrying cutting gear, breathing apparatus, ladders, axes and other rescue equipment is on constant alert.

Fueling the planes

The tarmac of an airport is a constant scene of bustling aircraft tugs, pulling and pushing planes into place. Fuel trucks which can carry up to 24,000 gallons (90,000 liters) pump fuel into the planes' greedy tanks. Big airplanes like the Boeing 747 have such a large fuel capacity that airports are now putting in fuel HYDRANTS linked by underground pipes to a large central fuel store. With this system, more than 600 gallons (2250 liters) a minute can be pumped through.

The security check

At most airports, an important part of the procedure is the security check. This is now usually carried out at a central point for all flights. Passengers' hand luggage goes through X-ray machines which can detect metal objects such as guns or knives. The passengers themselves go through a metal-detecting gateway. An ELECTROMAGNETIC FIELD passes between the doorposts of this gateway. If a passenger has any metal objects on his person the magnetic field is broken and this sets off an alarm. If the alarm is set off, a security guard with a hand-held METAL DETECTOR makes a further check of the passenger. Usually he finds the metal to be nothing more dangerous than a bunch of keys.

People movers

Most large jets need a bay approximately 300 feet (90 meters) wide. So, if ten of them are docked wing-tip to wing-tip, passengers must walk almost a mile to reach the farthest. Many airports have attempted to solve this problem by putting in moving sidewalks like flat escalators.

Other airports no longer have their planes docked in a long line. They have "satellite" terminals. These buildings stand apart from the main terminal and are linked to it by underground passageways or moving walkways. In this type of airport, all boarding gates can be a much shorter distance from the main terminal.

In other airports, instead of using moving walkways, people are taken from the main terminal to the aircraft boarding gates by "people movers." These are driverless, rubber-tired vehicles which move along a guideway.

Special buses are also used in airports such as Dulles International, Washington. These buses are like small lounges, hold 150 people and can be raised to the aircraft door so that people can walk straight onto the plane.

See also: **AIR TRAFFIC CONTROL, AVIONICS, RADAR, X-RAYS**

Airships

Until a few years ago, it seemed that airships were gone forever. They were dangerous and slow, and too many unfortunate accidents made people afraid to travel in them. Now a new generation of airships is coming along which are even cheaper to build and run than airplanes.

An airship is any aircraft like a balloon which is lighter than air, has an engine and can be steered. The gasbag or envelope which lifts the airship is filled with hydrogen or helium, which are both lighter than air.

Types of airship

There have been three kinds of airship: the nonrigid, the semirigid and the rigid. The nonrigid airship has no framework in the gas envelope to keep its shape. The gas is pumped into the envelope to a pressure which is greater than the pressure of the air outside. This holds the envelope in shape. The nose of the craft is, however, often strengthened to prevent the wind from flattening it when the craft is moving forward.

The lift in early airships was controlled by letting out gas and replacing it with air. This was wasteful because there was less and less lift as more and more gas was lost. These early craft also carried water BALLAST which was dropped when the crew wanted to go higher.

Nonrigid airships

Nonrigid airships (blimps) keep their shape by the pressure of the lifting gas in the bag, but the volume of the gas in the bag varies at different heights. This is because the air pressure grows less and less the higher the craft rises.

A way was found to keep the gas pressure constant by using ballonets. These were bags inside the envelope which were filled with air. As the airship rose, the lifting gas expanded. The air in the ballonets was then let out to allow for this. As the airship came down, the lifting gas contracted again. Then more air was pumped into the ballonets to take up the extra space. There were usually two ballonets in the forward end of the airship and two in the rear so that the balance of the craft could be adjusted.

Semirigid airships

The semirigid airship is similar to the nonrigid type, except that it has a metal keel along the whole length of the envelope. The Italian airship *Roma*, sold to the United States in 1920, was a craft of this type. It was 410 feet (125 meters) long, had six engines and a top speed of 68 mph (110 km/h).

The rigid airship

In the rigid airship, the envelope is supported by a stiff framework of aluminum girders. The gas is in 15 to 20 balloons inside the frame. The most famous rigid airships were the German *Zeppelins*, named after Graf von Zeppelin, who had watched balloons being used in the American Civil War. The British *R101* was also rigid. Built in 1929, it was 769 feet (234 meters) long, and it gave a top speed of 80 mph (129 km/h).

Right, above: Diagrams showing the difference between rigid and nonrigid airships. The only strengthening in the nonrigid airship is in the nose.

Right: The British *Skyship 500* moored to its mobile mast. The mast can be mounted on a truck, allowing the airship to be transported anywhere. The *500* can therefore fly from any site.

Left: The giant *Hindenburg* burns at Lakehurst, New Jersey.

The airship story

When the balloon was invented in 1783, people almost immediately began to think up ways of making it travel against the wind. The main problem was to find an engine that was light enough and powerful enough. The French engineer Henri Giffard built a 3-horsepower steam engine and this was fitted to a balloon filled with hydrogen. The 144 feet (44 meters) long machine took off from the Hippodrome in Paris in 1852, and flew successfully at 6 mph (10 km/h).

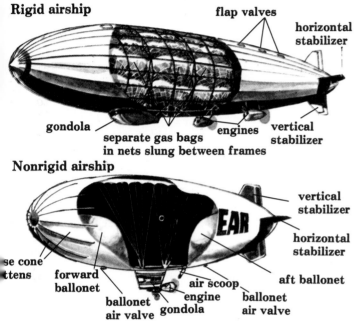

Rigid airship

flap valves

horizontal stabilizer

gondola

separate gas bags in nets slung between frames

engines

vertical stabilizer

Nonrigid airship

EAR

vertical stabilizer

horizontal stabilizer

se cone
ttens

forward ballonet

air scoop
engine
gondola

aft ballonet

ballonet air valve

ballonet air valve

In 1884 the French built another airship, *La France*. Its 9-horsepower electric motor gave a speed of 15 mph (24 km/h).

Then, in 1900, Count Ferdinand von Zeppelin built his first airship, the *LZ-1*. It had a rigid frame, supported inside by 16 aluminum hoops joined by wire stays. It was a great success. The German airship was powered by two 15-horsepower Daimler gasoline engines which drove it at a speed of 26 mph (42 km/h). In 1912 a similar airship carried 23 passengers on a flight lasting 7½ hours. The Germans were in the lead in airship-building. They were, therefore, well prepared to use these new machines for military purposes when World War I broke out in 1914.

The British realized that the main use of the airship was for checking out enemy territory. They therefore built some small, nonrigid craft (blimps) which were useful for finding and attacking enemy submarines. At the end of the war in 1918, Britain had a fleet of 103 of these blimps, while Germany had 68 rigid airships.

Some famous airships

In 1919 the British airship *R34* became the first airship to cross the Atlantic. Seven years later, in 1926, the explorer Roald Amundsen made the first flight over the North Pole in the Italian-built *Norge*. Epic flights such as these encouraged airship development.

In 1928 the German *Graf Zeppelin* began a successful service which included almost 150 Atlantic crossings. Eight years later the massive Zeppelin *Hindenburg* began a regular commercial air service across the Atlantic. However, the great days of the airship were soon to end in a series of disasters.

G-BIHN
AIRSHIP INDUSTRIES

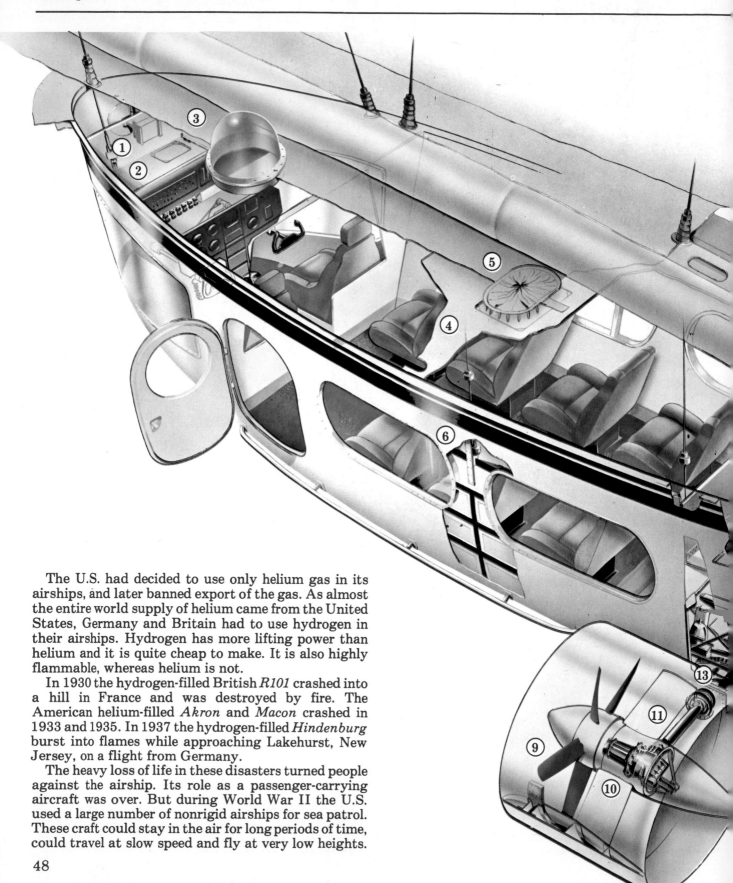

The U.S. had decided to use only helium gas in its airships, and later banned export of the gas. As almost the entire world supply of helium came from the United States, Germany and Britain had to use hydrogen in their airships. Hydrogen has more lifting power than helium and it is quite cheap to make. It is also highly flammable, whereas helium is not.

In 1930 the hydrogen-filled British *R101* crashed into a hill in France and was destroyed by fire. The American helium-filled *Akron* and *Macon* crashed in 1933 and 1935. In 1937 the hydrogen-filled *Hindenburg* burst into flames while approaching Lakehurst, New Jersey, on a flight from Germany.

The heavy loss of life in these disasters turned people against the airship. Its role as a passenger-carrying aircraft was over. But during World War II the U.S. used a large number of nonrigid airships for sea patrol. These craft could stay in the air for long periods of time, could travel at slow speed and fly at very low heights.

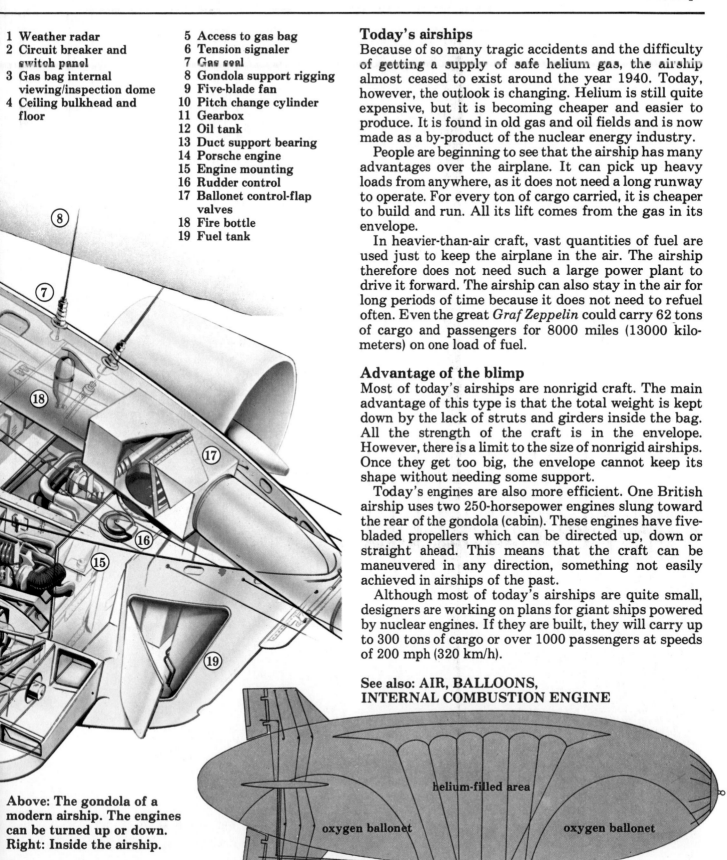

1 Weather radar
2 Circuit breaker and switch panel
3 Gas bag internal viewing/inspection dome
4 Ceiling bulkhead and floor
5 Access to gas bag
6 Tension signaler
7 Gas seal
8 Gondola support rigging
9 Five-blade fan
10 Pitch change cylinder
11 Gearbox
12 Oil tank
13 Duct support bearing
14 Porsche engine
15 Engine mounting
16 Rudder control
17 Ballonet control-flap valves
18 Fire bottle
19 Fuel tank

Today's airships

Because of so many tragic accidents and the difficulty of getting a supply of safe helium gas, the airship almost ceased to exist around the year 1940. Today, however, the outlook is changing. Helium is still quite expensive, but it is becoming cheaper and easier to produce. It is found in old gas and oil fields and is now made as a by-product of the nuclear energy industry.

People are beginning to see that the airship has many advantages over the airplane. It can pick up heavy loads from anywhere, as it does not need a long runway to operate. For every ton of cargo carried, it is cheaper to build and run. All its lift comes from the gas in its envelope.

In heavier-than-air craft, vast quantities of fuel are used just to keep the airplane in the air. The airship therefore does not need such a large power plant to drive it forward. The airship can also stay in the air for long periods of time because it does not need to refuel often. Even the great *Graf Zeppelin* could carry 62 tons of cargo and passengers for 8000 miles (13000 kilometers) on one load of fuel.

Advantage of the blimp

Most of today's airships are nonrigid craft. The main advantage of this type is that the total weight is kept down by the lack of struts and girders inside the bag. All the strength of the craft is in the envelope. However, there is a limit to the size of nonrigid airships. Once they get too big, the envelope cannot keep its shape without needing some support.

Today's engines are also more efficient. One British airship uses two 250-horsepower engines slung toward the rear of the gondola (cabin). These engines have five-bladed propellers which can be directed up, down or straight ahead. This means that the craft can be maneuvered in any direction, something not easily achieved in airships of the past.

Although most of today's airships are quite small, designers are working on plans for giant ships powered by nuclear engines. If they are built, they will carry up to 300 tons of cargo or over 1000 passengers at speeds of 200 mph (320 km/h).

See also: AIR, BALLOONS, INTERNAL COMBUSTION ENGINE

Above: The gondola of a modern airship. The engines can be turned up or down. Right: Inside the airship.

helium-filled area

oxygen ballonet

oxygen ballonet

Air Traffic Control

Around an airport the air can be full of planes of different sizes, traveling in all directions at various speeds and heights. It is the air traffic controller's job to see that all these aircraft land and take off safely.

During long-distance flights, when there are few planes about, the pilot uses the navigational aids in his own aircraft. He flies at a fixed height and no other aircraft is allowed within about 5 miles (8 kilometers) of him in any direction. Nor are there any planes within 1000 feet (300 meters) above or below him. As he flies across country he comes under the control of different air traffic control centers. Each center hands him on to the next center on his flight plan. The plane is on the radar screen of some air traffic controller all the way through its flight.

However, as soon as he approaches a busy area, the pilot enters a control zone. While in this area he must follow a certain course at a given speed and height. These are given to him by the air traffic controller.

The air traffic controller

The air traffic controller makes the decisions. Only he has all the information about all the aircraft inside his zone. He must keep all the planes in his zone a certain distance apart, both vertically and horizontally. He also decides the order of planes taking off and landing from that airport.

The controller needs information about all the aircraft in his area. He must know a plane's height and position, whether it is coming in to land or if it is just passing by, and, of course, he must know the identity of each plane.

Each flight needs a flight plan which is prepared by the pilot before he takes off. This plan gives the plane's identification, its airport of departure and destination, estimated time of arrival, its route and cruising height. This is the information that is sent ahead to the air traffic controllers.

The controller keeps in touch with the aircraft in his zone by VHF (very high frequency) radio. This has a range of about 200 miles (320 kilometers) when the aircraft is at a high altitude.

Wind speed and direction, height of clouds, and temperature are fed to the controller from local centers. He must also know the visibility on the runway.

Radar control

The modern air traffic controller's job would be impossible without radar. The radar scanning antenna (you may have seen them going round and round at an airport) can pick up the position of all planes at up to 300 miles (480 kilometers) distant. But airfield control radars usually work at a shorter range—perhaps 100 miles (160 kilometers). On the radar screen, aircraft show up as small "blips" or crosses. The distance of the aircraft from the airport is indicated by its distance from the center of the screen, and its bearing by the angle to the center. This kind of radar system is called PPI (Plan Position Indicator).

One problem with radar is that it will receive signals from objects other than aircraft. Heavy rain or snow, for example, will produce "smears" on the screen. It is possible, however, to cut out unwanted signals from objects that do not move. Only moving objects such as aircraft appear on the radar screen in modern installations.

To cut out as much interference as possible, radar antennas are not always at the airport itself. They can be positioned on high ground where they get a good "clean" view of the airspace all around.

Stacking

Many aircraft approach an airport at about the same time, sometimes in poor visibility. As the planes travel at different speeds and the pilots cannot see one another, the air traffic controller must keep them at safe distances. He does this by directing the planes into a "stack." A stack is a number of planes circling in an oval pattern, one above the other, with 1000 feet (300 meters) of height between them. As the plane at the

Left: A picture of London's Heathrow airport as seen on the airfield surface radar screen. Individual aircraft can be clearly seen. The radar antenna is on the central control tower. Surface radar is used to keep aircraft apart and prevent collisions on the ground.

Above: On the radar director's screen each airplane shows up as a cross with its number, height and destination. An instrument on the airplane itself sends these details out automatically when it picks up the radar beam from the airport. Modern radar systems are controlled by computers.

Far left: A constant watch is kept on every aircraft in the air traffic controller's area from this control tower. The controller makes sure that every plane has room to land. If the runway is slippery or wet, the planes have to brake gently and will need more time to slow down.

Did you know?

O'Hare International Airport in Chicago is the busiest in the world. The staff handles about 800,000 takeoffs and landings in a year—an average of more than one every minute, day and night. This adds up to more than 45 million passengers—twice the entire population of California!

bottom of the stack begins its final approach to the runway, each plane above it is told to come down to the next level. Eventually all the aircraft in the stack are cleared into the airport.

Landing by instruments

The controller usually takes the pilot up to the final approach to the runway. Then the pilot can switch to the ILS (Instrument Landing System). This system sends out radio beams so that the aircraft can line itself up with the runway and come in on the right path. Two radio beams are sent out. One guides the plane in on the correct compass bearing; the other keeps it at the correct height.

When the plane's instruments pick up the ILS beams, two markers appear on the pilot's artificial horizon instrument. Two other needles, called flight director indicators, also appear on the same instrument. These markers and needles show the pilot where the plane is in the ILS beams, so that he can follow the beams down to the runway.

Blind landing

Most planes today have blind landing equipment. This is to help when landing in fog or other bad weather conditions. With this equipment, the pilot does not have to make corrections to keep his plane on the ILS beam—a computer does the job for him. The pilot merely brings his speed down and from then on the computer adjusts the throttle and other flying instruments automatically. Most pilots prefer to bring the plane down themselves.

Runway lights

When the runway comes into view, the pilot sees a pattern of lights. The approach to the runway is indicated by a special pattern. This has a white or green centerline crossed by white bars which get narrower as the runway approaches. The runway itself has white centerline lights and white bars to mark the touchdown area. At the end of the runway the centerline is red.

The Visual Approach Slope Indicator (VASI) lights are on either side of the touchdown point. This system is quite simple. It consists of two sets of lights fitted with reflectors which shine through narrow slits so that the beams are very narrow. One set of lights is red, the other white. The angle of the white lights is slightly higher than that of the reds. These lights are carefully lined up so that when the pilot approaches at the right slope he sees one red light and one white light on each

Below: The ILS (Instrument Landing System) uses narrow radio beams to guide aircraft down to land. The localizer beam (shown in orange on the diagram) is horizontal. It keeps the pilot at the right approach angle. The glidepath beam is vertical (shown yellow on the diagram). It keeps the pilot at the correct height as he approaches.

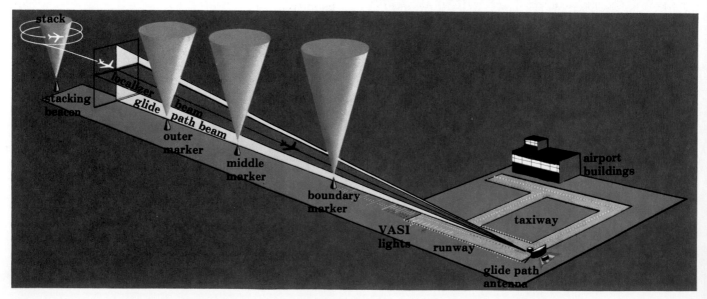

Left and below: Visual Approach Slope Indicator (VASI) keeps the pilot on the right path as he nears the runway. There are two sets of lights fitted with reflectors that send out red and white lights in narrow beams. If the pilot sees all white lights, he is too high; if all red lights, he is too low. One red and one white light each side of the runway and he is coming in at the right slope.

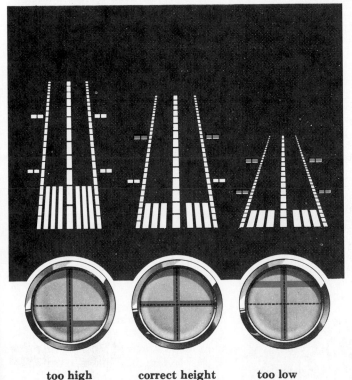

| too high | correct height | too low |

side of the runway. If he is too high he will see white lights only; if too low, only red lights. The pilot keeps to the centerline of the runway with both red and white lights showing, and lands safely.

If anything goes wrong on the runway, the controller tells the pilot to overshoot. At the decision height —usually about 200 feet (60 meters)—the pilot opens the throttle and pulls the control column back to overshoot the runway and climb to safety.

The controller also makes sure that each plane has room to land. Some planes leave more turbulence (disturbed air) behind them than others, so the planes must not be too close. If the runway is slippery or wet, the plane has to brake more gently when landing, and needs more time to clear the runway.

When the plane is down, the controller directs it to the correct runway exit for parking and so the passengers can get off.

Thanks to all these safety precautions, flying has become a very safe form of transport. It is now much safer to fly in a modern airliner than it is to cross the main street in your home town.

See also: AIRPLANE, AIRPORT, ANTENNAS, AVIATION HISTORY, FLIGHT RECORDER, RADAR, RADIO

Alkalis

Alkalis are among the most useful of chemicals. Millions of tons of them are used in industry every year. When alkalis are dissolved in water they are very bitter to the taste and feel soapy. The word alkali comes from the Arabic word meaning "ashes." Plant ashes were the first known source of alkalis and in ancient times people used the ashes of plants to make soap.

Strong alkalis are dangerous chemicals and are called caustic because they burn the skin. Caustic soda and caustic potash are the best known alkalis. Their chemical names are sodium hydroxide and potassium hydroxide. Alkalis are BASES that will dissolve in water. A base is a substance that combines with acid to form a SALT plus water only. The solution will turn LITMUS PAPER blue.

Uses of alkalis

The most important use of alkalis is in making soap. Caustic soda is most used for this purpose. It is also used in the making of rayon yarn. Alkalis have many other uses in industry. They play an important part in the making of paper, detergents, water softeners, glass, bicarbonate of soda and household ammonia.

The alkali metals

The alkali metals are sodium, lithium, francium, rubidium, cesium and potassium. These metals form some of the common alkalis when they react with water. Other substances, such as ammonia and calcium, form alkalis too.

All the alkali metals are very light and silvery-white in color. They can all be cut with a knife and they react violently when they touch water, giving out hydrogen gas and heat. They will all react with water vapor in the air. These metals must, therefore, be kept stored under oil or in special sealed containers.

Pure sodium is used in the sodium lamps we see along some of our highways. It is also used to conduct heat energy away from nuclear reactors.

Lithium is used in some processes for refining metals and in making alloys. It is also used as a special-purpose LUBRICANT. Francium is a RADIOACTIVE element.

Rubidium and cesium vary according to the light falling on them. This makes them suitable for use in photoelectric cells. Potassium is a vital plant food.

Alkali metals are never found in the pure state in the earth. They can be separated from their impurities by electrolysis.

See also: ACIDS, AMMONIA, ELECTROLYSIS, SOAPS AND DETERGENTS

Above: Lithium is the lightest metal. The polished crystal is a complex aluminum silicate which is a useful source of the alkali metal lithium.

Left: When lithium is heated it gives out a red light. In fireworks, a small amount of lithium nitrate is added to the mixture of chemicals to give the red effect.

Allergy

Most of us know someone who suffers from hay fever at certain times of the year, or someone who breaks out in hives after eating raspberries or strawberries. Some people have difficulty breathing when they get close to dogs or cats. All these people are suffering from an allergy.

An allergy is a body reaction that occurs in people who are sensitive to certain substances. About one person in seven in the United States suffers from some kind of allergy. The most common allergies are hay fever, asthma, eczema (itchy patches on the skin), hives and some kinds of headaches. Allergies can also cause stomach upsets.

It used to be thought that hay fever was caused by pollen in hay. We now know that it can be caused by pollen from many kinds of grasses and trees. The pollen is blown around in the air in early summer or fall.

Anyone who suffers from hay fever will recognize the symptoms. This person probably has sore, itchy eyes, a runny or congested nose and spends a lot of time sneezing.

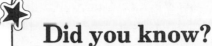

Did you know?

If both parents have an allergy, each of their children has about a 75 percent chance of having an allergy too. The children's allergy is not necessarily the same as that of their parents.

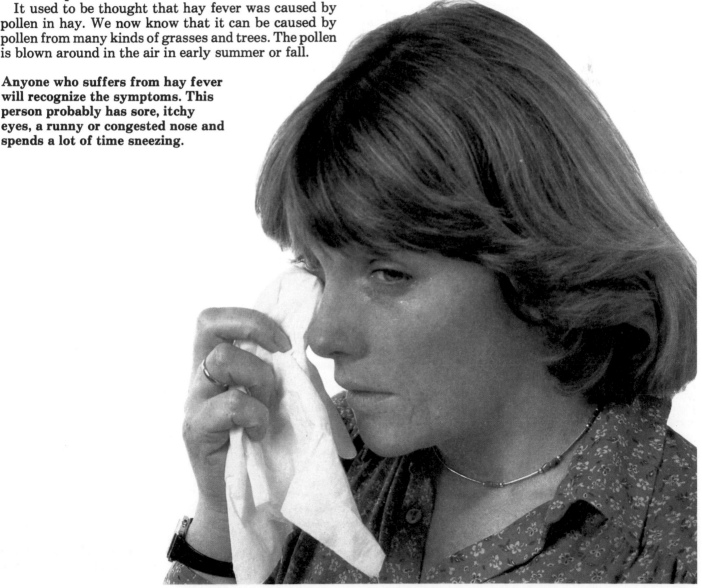

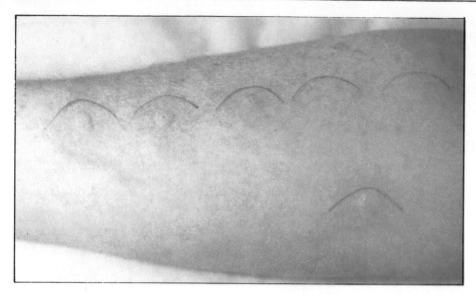

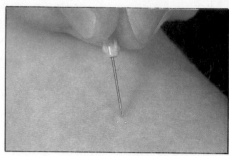

Above: The skin of the arm is pricked in several places and small amounts of possible allergen are added to see if there is a reaction. The positive reaction is shown in the red bump (left). The other marks show no sign of a reaction.

What causes an allergy?

Allergies are caused by substances called allergens. These allergens spark off certain symptoms in people who are sensitive to them. Among the most common allergens are pollen, fish, eggs, milk, insect bites, cosmetics, drugs and animal hair.

A common allergen in the home is the dust mite, a tiny creature which lives in rugs, bedclothes and drapes. Heat, cold and sunlight can also act like allergens to some people.

Most people who suffer from an allergy come from a family in which their parents or other close relatives have had allergies of some kind. Doctors do not understand why this is so; in fact, they are still very puzzled as to why certain people suffer from allergies and others do not.

How an allergy starts

When an allergen enters the body of an allergic person—when pollen gets up the nose of someone who suffers from hay fever, for instance—that person's body produces ANTIBODIES. A different antibody is produced for each allergen. The allergens and antibodies then get together to produce substances called HISTAMINES. These histamines seem to be responsible for all the sneezing and tearing of the hay fever sufferer, and other symptoms of allergies.

There is histamine in all animals and vegetables. It is quite harmless while it remains enclosed inside one particular type of the body's cells. But when it is released it triggers off all kinds of reactions. One reaction is that the speed of the blood flowing through our blood vessels decreases. This causes a small quantity of blood to seep through the blood vessel walls, causing swelling. When this happens in a person's nose as a result of breathing in pollen, all the

inside of the nose becomes swollen and irritated. He sneezes—he has "hay fever."

Treating allergies

Doctors usually advise people with allergies to avoid the substances to which they are allergic. When a person is allergic to a certain kind of food, this is quite easy. But it is almost impossible to avoid such things as dust and pollen.

When pollen is suspected, the doctor may give the patient a prick test. The doctor or nurse gently pricks the patient's arm with a needle, then drops a watery liquid on the pricked spot. The liquid contains a small amount of one particular allergen. As many as 40 of these little tests may be performed in one session.

If the patient is allergic to one of the allergens, a red bump will show up at the spot where that allergen was dropped.

When the doctor discovers which pollen the patient is allergic to, he may then start a course of injections. These injections contain small amounts of the allergen and their aim is to encourage the patient's body to produce a harmless "blocking antibody." This kind of antibody gets in the way of the allergen before it can set off the patient's symptoms. Courses of these injections can be given before the pollen season begins. They work successfully on about three-fourths of sufferers.

There are also several kinds of drugs that are given to allergy sufferers. Perhaps the best known of these are the ANTIHISTAMINES. These drugs help to reduce the symptoms caused by the histamine.

There are drugs that can be given to people with food allergies too. But doctors usually just tell the patient to avoid eating the foods which cause their allergy.

See also: BLOOD, CELLS

Alloys

We usually talk about metal objects as though they were made of pure metal, such as aluminum, iron or tin. Very few of these articles are actually pure metal. Most of them are mixtures of two or more metals, or of a metal and some other material. These mixtures are called alloys.

A knife made of pure iron would be a very useless object. It could never be sharp because iron is a soft metal. But a knife blade made of iron that has been mixed with carbon and other elements will remain hard and sharp for a long time. A pan made of pure aluminum would wear away quickly because it would be too soft. One made of aluminum that has been mixed with copper can be used for years because it is much harder.

The number of possible alloys is almost endless. Two metals can be mixed in hundreds of different proportions to make alloys with very different characteristics. The value of alloys over pure metals lies in the great variety of blends that can be made. New alloys are constantly being made as technology advances and different kinds of metals are needed in industries that make automobiles, aircraft and space hardware.

Making alloys

Making alloys can sometimes be quite a difficult process. The easiest way is to melt the ingredients together in the correct proportions. However, this is not always possible. The melting points of metals are very different, so one with a lower melting point will boil away before the other metal has had time to melt.

This happens, for instance, when making brass from a mixture of copper and zinc. Copper melts at a much higher temperature (1982 degrees F [1084 degrees C]) than zinc. If the copper and zinc are heated together to 1982 degrees F in order to melt the copper, the liquid

Above: Iron being poured from a furnace into a ladle containing nickel and magnesium. This mixture makes a very strong alloy.

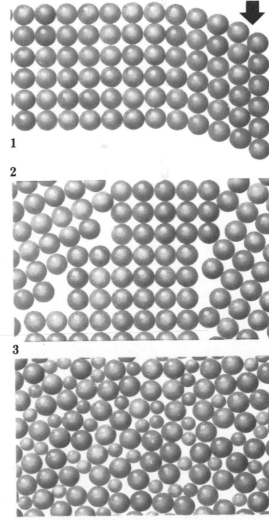

Below right: Alloys are often much stronger than the original metals which are mixed. A pure metal bends easily because its atoms are in straight rows (1). Dislocations between rows of atoms allow splits to form (2). When another metal is added, the odd-sized atoms break up the rows and toughen the metal (3).

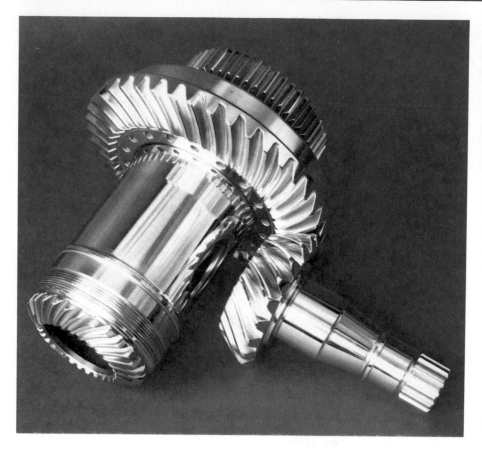

Above: Diecasting is used to make complex metal parts. It needs an alloy which will flow well into a mold. The casting is taken from the mold and then cooled in water. Left: Various alloys are chosen for different purposes. These gear wheels have to stand up to the high loads between the crown wheel and pinion.

zinc has already boiled at this temperature and EVAPORATED into the air. So to make brass, the copper is heated by itself until it melts, then the solid zinc is added. The zinc dissolves quickly in the liquid copper and does not have time to evaporate very much.

Bronze
This mixture of copper and tin was probably discovered by accident about 3000 BC. The discovery was so important that it gave its name to one of the prehistoric ages—the Bronze Age. Bronze is a mixture of roughly 10 parts of copper to one of tin. It is harder than either copper or tin alone, and was used for making swords and other weapons before iron was discovered. Bronze has long been used for making large bells because of its rich tone when struck. It is also used for making statues. In industry, the bearings of heavy machines are often made of phosphor bronze; a bronze to which a small amount of phosphorus has been added to make the alloy harder.

Brass
Another copper alloy, brass has between 10 percent and 45 percent zinc by weight. Small quantities of other metals may be added for special purposes. The brass from which cartridges are made contains only 30 percent zinc. The alloy is therefore soft enough to allow the cartridge cases to be stamped out from the cold metal. Brasses containing more than 36 percent zinc are hard and strong. Brass may wear out slowly, but it does not rust, so it has long been used for water faucets and other items, like propellers, which come in contact with water.

Cast iron
This is impure iron. It has, in addition to iron, between 2 percent and 4.5 percent of carbon plus very small quantities of manganese, phosphorus, silicon and sulfur. It is cheap and can take great stress. Cast iron is used for making engine blocks.

Steel
In addition to iron, this alloy has less than 2 percent of carbon, less than 1 percent manganese and even smaller amounts of silicon, phosphorus, sulfur and oxygen. Steel is stronger than iron and there are thousands of different types. These are different because of the different chemicals which are added to the iron, or because of the way the steel is heated and cooled during its making.

An automobile may have over a hundred different kinds of steel in its engine and body.

Stainless steel

The steel most often found in the home. It is an alloy of iron with 18 percent chromium in it. This metal forms a tough film on the surface of the steel which protects the iron in the steel from rusting. Stainless steel also has 8 percent nickel which allows the alloy to be easily worked. The main uses for stainless steel in the home are for knives, sinks and pans. It is also used a great deal in the aircraft and automobile industries, as well as in hospitals and food-producing plants.

Aluminum alloys

These are used when strong, light material is needed, particularly in the aircraft and space industries. Copper, magnesium and silicon are added to the aluminum, often with small quantities of manganese, zinc, titanium and nickel. One of the first aluminum alloys was Duralumin, a tough, light and strong material used in the old Zeppelin airships. Duralumin had 4 percent copper. It is only slightly heavier than pure aluminum, but is nearly as strong as steel.

Lead alloys

The most important of these is a mixture of lead and antimony. Lead-antimony alloys are used in making bullets.

Gold and silver are also made into alloys. This makes the precious metals harder and prevents them wearing away as quickly as they would otherwise do. Yellow gold is an alloy of about 9 parts of gold and 1 of copper. It is used for dental fillings and jewelry. Sterling silver, used for tableware, is about 92 percent silver and 8 percent copper.

Pewter

An alloy made from tin with the addition of copper, lead and antimony. Usually between 75 and 80 percent of pewter is tin. During the 17th and 18th centuries people in Europe used pewter household utensils. It is not used for this purpose today as it tarnishes quickly and does not stand heat well.

Some alloys must be very resistant to electric current so that they can produce electric light and heat. An alloy of tungsten and thorium is used to make the FILAMENTS of electric light bulbs. Heating units for electric stoves and toasters are made of nickel-chromium alloys. These alloys can stand great heat without burning out. The opposite of these resistant alloys is copper, one of the few metals used in an almost pure state. Copper allows an electric current to flow through it very easily.

Amalgam

An alloy of mercury with some other metal. Unlike mercury, however, amalgams are solid. They are hard enough to be used in dental fillings. Like mercury, amalgams are bright and silvery. At one time they were used to silver mirrors.

Some alloys are useful because they melt at very low temperatures. If tin, lead, bismuth and cadmium are mixed in the right proportions, the alloy melts at only 71 degrees F (22 degrees C). Alloys like this are used for automatic water-sprinklers in buildings. Should a fire break out, the alloy melts, and the sprinklers start.

Solder

Another alloy which melts easily, solder is used to join other metal surfaces together. Solder must melt more easily than the two metals on which it is used. It is silvery in color because it is usually made of lead and tin in varying amounts. Some solders contain small quantities of silver or other metals.

New alloys are being developed all the time to meet the needs of modern technology. Titanium, for instance, a metal which combines great strength with lightness, is used in alloys for building spacecraft.

See also: BEARINGS, BELLS, LIGHT BULB

The picture below shows a process for refining alloys. An ingot of the alloy (the large silver cylinder) is lowered into a bath of molten slag which will react with the metal. An electric current is passed through the ingot. This melts the ingot and allows the purified alloy to collect at the bottom of the bath.

Aluminum

Aluminum is sometimes called the magic metal. This is because it can be made into so many different things, from the bodies and wings of airliners to pots and pans, from the upper decks of large ships to chewing gum wrappers.

Aluminum is useful for several reasons. It is very light and weighs only a third as much as iron and steel. Pure, silvery-white aluminum is soft, but when it is mixed with other metals (alloyed) it becomes as strong as steel.

Because it is soft, the metal can be drawn out to make thin wire. A few ounces of aluminum can be drawn out so thinly that there would be enough wire to stretch right across the United States.

The metal CONDUCTS electricity easily. Pure aluminum wire, strengthened by steel cable, is used to carry electric currents over long distances. Aluminum is also non-magnetic—it cannot be magnetized. This makes it useful in some kinds of electrical equipment.

Apart from its strength and lightness, aluminum is also very useful because it does not rust like iron and steel. It is especially useful for making pots and pans because it will not contaminate the food, and it holds heat well. Sheets of aluminum foil are used for wrapping food because it is greaseproof and keeps out moisture.

Aluminum's raw material

There is more aluminum in the earth's crust than any other metal; in fact, 7 percent of all the material in the earth's crust is aluminum. But the metal is never found in its pure state; it is always mixed with other elements. No one has ever dug up a piece of aluminum.

Nearly all the aluminum we use comes from an ORE called bauxite. It is so called because large amounts were first found at a place called Les Baux in France. Bauxite is usually mined from hard rock formations, but it can also be as soft as mud. The main bauxite-producing countries are the United States, Australia, Jamaica, France, the USSR, Guyana and Guinea. Most aluminum comes from bauxite that contains 50 percent alumina (aluminum oxide). It takes about 4 pounds of bauxite to make 2 pounds of alumina. This will make 1 pound of aluminum.

How aluminum is made

Bauxite is quite cheap. Separating aluminum from the other materials in the ore, however, is an expensive process. This is because the process needs vast amounts of electricity. Therefore, aluminum plants are often located where there is hydroelectric power rather

Above: Electric current passes through red-hot carbon electrodes to extract pure aluminum from the molten alumina solution.

Right: Mining bauxite by the opencast method. Thousands of tons of bauxite are scooped up daily by giant machines.

Above: The liquid aluminum is poured into molds. It is now pure enough for most industrial uses.

Left: A line of pots—the furnaces in which the metal is purified. The curved strips carry an electric current to the anode blocks. The large pipes carry off waste gases.

than where the bauxite is mined—British Columbia, the Alps and Scandinavia, for example.

At the bauxite mines, the ore is crushed before being shipped to the aluminum factories. The factories grind the ore again until it is a fine powder. Then the impurities must be separated from the powdered ore.

To do this bauxite powder is mixed with hot caustic-soda solution and pumped into large pressure tanks called DIGESTERS. The temperature in the digester tanks is 300 degrees F (149 degrees C). In the tanks, the alumina dissolves but the impurities remain solid. These impurities are filtered out as "red mud."

The liquid that remains after the red mud has been filtered out is pumped into tall tanks called PRECIPITATORS. In these tanks, the liquid is allowed to cool slowly. The alumina precipitates (comes out of the liquid as crystals) as it cools. These crystals are then heated until they are white hot to remove any water that remains in them. The result is a dry, white powder—the alumina. But we still do not have aluminum.

Alumina to aluminum

To turn the alumina into aluminum it has to be dissolved in a substance called CRYOLITE. This process takes place in a large steel bath or pot with a carbon lining. An electric current is passed through the pot from carbon ANODES that hang in the liquid from overhead bars. The current goes through the liquid to steel bars embedded in the carbon bottom of the pot (the cathode).

As the current goes through, the liquid breaks up and almost pure aluminum falls to the bottom of the pot. Waste gas is given off, and this has to be purified. The molten aluminum is siphoned off and cast into molds.

This process can go on continuously as long as alumina is added to the pot and aluminum is removed from time to time. One pot can produce as much as 1000 pounds (453 kilograms) of aluminum in 24 hours. Modern aluminum plants have several hundred pots, each holding perhaps 20 tons.

Very large amounts of electricity are used in this process. The electricity used by the average American family in a year would not produce more than a hundred pounds (45 kilograms) of aluminum.

Shaping aluminum

Aluminum from the pots goes to furnaces where other metals can be added to make aluminum alloys. The added metals can be zinc, copper, magnesium or others,

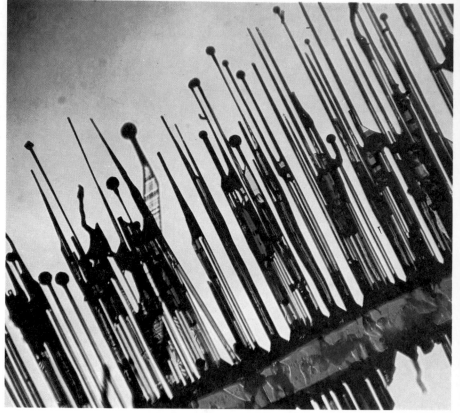

People knew aluminum oxides long before they managed to make aluminum. The picture above shows rubies (red aluminum oxide) in the raw state before they are cut and polished. On the right are sapphire whiskers (blue aluminum oxide) which were grown in the laboratory.

depending on the purpose of the finished alloy. The alloys are cast into ingots (molds shaped for easy storage).

Aluminum ingots can then be shaped in several ways. They can be rolled between giant steel rollers to make sheets less than ½ inch (1.3 centimeters) thick. They can be rolled still more and stretched until the aluminum is no more than .006 inch (.02 centimeter) thick—aluminum foil. Toothpaste tubes can also be made in this way.

Did you know?

In 1855 a Frenchman called Henri Sainte-Claire Deville entered a shiny piece of aluminum in the Paris Exhibition. Napoleon III was so impressed that he asked Sainte-Claire Deville to find a way of making the metal cheaply. No easy way could be found and the metal became more precious than gold. Napoleon is said to have had a set of aluminum cutlery made for his most honored guests.

The aluminum can also be extruded. This process is rather like squeezing toothpaste from a tube. The pieces of aluminum are cut into lengths and heated to about 830 degrees F (443 degrees C) to soften them. Than they are forced through a hole of the required shape and size. Aluminum door and window sections can be made in this way.

In forging aluminum, the metal is heated before being pressed into a die of the required shape.

Sand-cast aluminum is made by pouring the molten metal into a mold made of a clay-sand mixture. When the metal hardens, the mold is broken away and the aluminum metal is left in the required shape.

Aluminum wire can be drawn (pulled out) to a very fine size. Machines pull a rod of the metal through holes in hard steel. The holes are smaller than the rod. A drawing machine can make almost a mile of aluminum wire in a minute.

The history of aluminum

Aluminum was discovered quite recently in human history. In 1809 the Englishman, Sir Humphry Davy, produced aluminum oxide, but he could not make aluminum itself. It was Sir Humphry, however, who gave us the name "aluminium," a spelling still used in Britain and some other countries.

The first man to produce aluminum may have been

Hans Christian Oersted, a Danish chemist. He is thought to have made a tiny amount in 1825. We know for certain that Friedrich Wöhler of Germany made a small quantity of the metal in 1827.

In 1886, after much research, two men discovered a cheap way of making aluminum. They were Charles Martin Hall of Thompson, Ohio, and the Frenchman Paul Héroult. Neither man knew that the other was working on the aluminum problem. Their method became known as the Hall-Héroult process, and it is really the same process that is still used today.

Hall and Héroult each had the idea of dissolving the alumina in the mineral cryolite and passing an electric current through the electrolyte to produce aluminum. Both Hall and Héroult were 22 years of age when they made their discovery which grew into the giant aluminum industry which we know today. Iron is the only metal produced in greater quantity than aluminum.

The useful metal

Aluminum is used in an amazing variety of ways. Aircraft are made chiefly of this metal; so are spacecraft. The building and transportation industries are among the biggest users. Tiny flakes of the metal can be added to varnish to make aluminum paint. Steel is coated with a thin layer of aluminum to stop it rusting, and this is used for roofing, fencing and barbed wire. In the home, aluminum goes into cooking utensils, window frames and heating equipment. Aluminum is all around us.

See also: ALLOYS, ELECTRIC CURRENT, ELECTROLYSIS

Below: How aluminum is made. First, bauxite is "digested" in caustic soda, then filtered to remove impurities. Then it is heated to drive off water. The alumina that is left is mixed with cryolite in a large pot lined with carbon and an electric current is passed through it. Liquid aluminum forms at the bottom and is siphoned off.

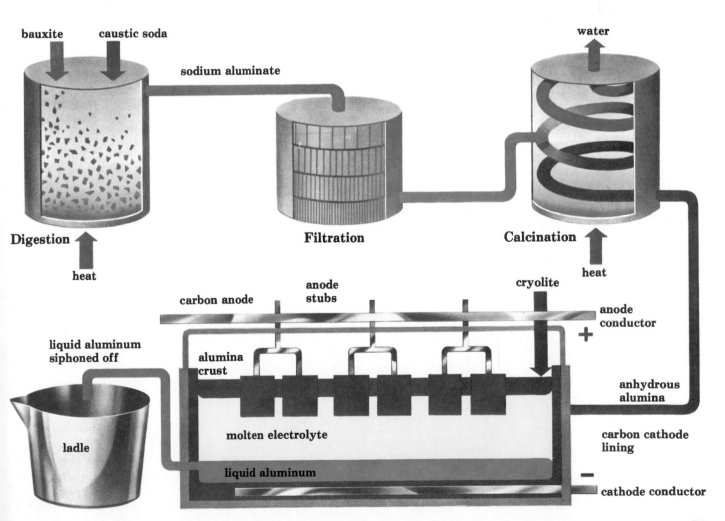

Amino Acids

Amino acids are often called the building blocks of life. They combine together to form proteins—the basic materials from which all living matter is made. There are only 20 types of amino acid, but they combine in many ways to form millions of kinds of protein.

Amino acids and health

Our bodies use up proteins all the time. They are lost through bodily waste, perspiration, the growth of hair and nails, and through other processes. As a result, the body needs a regular supply of new proteins. These are obtained by taking in food that contains proteins and breaking them down into amino acids. This takes place through the action of substances in the digestive system. The amino acids obtained in this way are recombined to form the kinds of proteins that the body requires. The proteins in our food cannot be used directly because the proteins found in animal and plant foodstuffs are different from those our bodies use.

All amino acids are made up from atoms of carbon, oxygen, hydrogen and nitrogen. The body can manufacture some amino acids from other substances, but there are eight amino acids that the body cannot make. Therefore, it is essential that these are present in the food that we eat. If any one of them is missing, a person's health will suffer. This is one reason why a carefully balanced diet is so important.

Life's variety

Just as the letters of the alphabet combine to form thousands of words, so the 20 amino acids combine to form thousands of proteins. These vary widely in size and function. They produce different species of plant and animal life. In each species, agents called GENES govern the way in which amino acids are combined. Individuals of the same species have different genes. So their amino acids are combined differently. This is what produces the characteristics that make one person different from another.

Proteins at work

Insulin is one of the group of proteins called HORMONES. These are often described as "chemical messengers." They carry substances that cause various activities to take place in our bodies. Insulin's vital function is to regulate the amount of glucose sugar in our blood. Most protein molecules contain hundreds or thousands of amino acid molecules. But insulin contains a mere 51; so insulin is referred to as a lightweight protein.

Many amino acid formations in our body produce proteins called enzymes. These substances, such as amylase and dehydrogenase, act as CATALYSTS. This means that they speed up certain chemical changes that take place in the body without undergoing permanent change themselves.

Another amino acid formation is collagen. This protein binds our bones, ligaments, cartilage, muscles and skin together. Swallowing and the movement of joints are aided by the body's natural lubricant.

Some proteins are involved in carrying various substances around the body. They are able to bind molecules together and carry them along in the

Below and right: This diagram illustrates the formation of proteins from amino acids. There are 20 types of amino acid from which protein is made. As shown, the structure of any amino acid can be represented by a combination of hydrogen, nitrogen, carbon and oxygen atoms, with another group that is variable (labeled R in the diagram). In joining, a pair of acid molecules form a peptide bond (1) by losing a water molecule (2). Numerous links of this kind form a polypeptide chain (3), or protein, which coils (4) and forms a helix (spiral). The different types of amino acids can combine in thousands of combinations. Each combination is a different protein.

Protein construction

additional amino acids

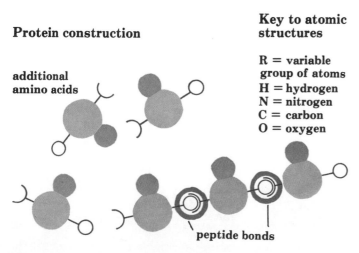

peptide bonds

Key to atomic structures

R = variable group of atoms
H = hydrogen
N = nitrogen
C = carbon
O = oxygen

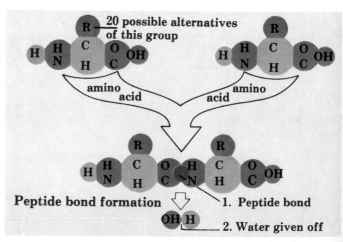

Peptide bond formation
1. Peptide bond
2. Water given off

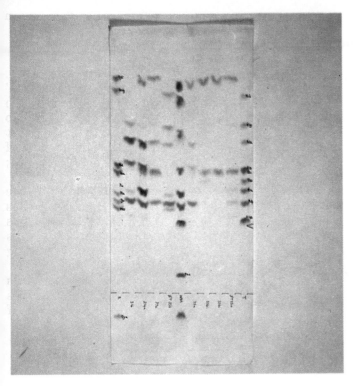

Left: The amino acids that make up proteins can be separated and identified by a special process. The protein molecules are split up by chemical means. Then they are dissolved in a weak acid and put onto a filter paper. An electric current, passed through the damp paper, separates the amino acids. They are carried different distances across the paper. After separation, the amino acids can be identified.

bloodstream, or across the membranes into the cells. One of the most important of these is hemoglobin, the red pigment in the blood. It carries oxygen from the lungs to other parts of the body.

IMMUNOGLOBULINS, or antibody molecules, are protective proteins. They appear in our blood to help us fight the effects of foreign bodies, such as pollen. Immunoglobulins also help people to counteract the effects of eating food to which they are allergic.

Besides carrying out various active roles, proteins also act as the body's emergency energy supply when we are not eating enough of the right food.

See also: ACIDS, ALLERGY, ATOMS AND MOLECULES, BLOOD, DIGESTIVE SYSTEM, PROTEINS

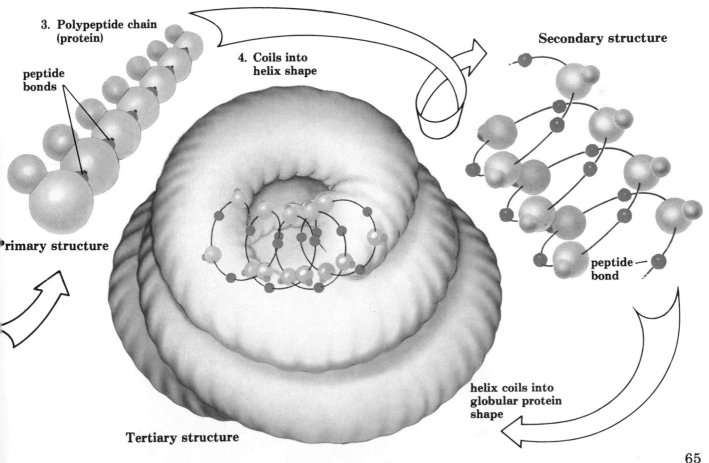

3. Polypeptide chain (protein)

peptide bonds

Primary structure

4. Coils into helix shape

Secondary structure

peptide bond

Tertiary structure

helix coils into globular protein shape

Ammonia

The liquid we see inside bottles labeled "household ammonia" is not really ammonia at all. Ammonia is an invisible gas at room temperature, but if it is cooled it becomes a colorless liquid. Household ammonia is ammonia dissolved in water—ammonium hydroxide, a cleaning fluid.

Ammonia is made up of one part of nitrogen and three parts of hydrogen, giving its chemical symbol NH_3. Small quantities are made in nature by the decaying of animal and vegetable matter. It has a very strong, sharp odor and is an alkali.

The high priests of ancient Egypt knew about ammonia. They prepared it from camel dung. In the Middle Ages it was made from the antlers of deer and called "spirits of hartshorn."

Nowadays, ammonia is a most useful chemical. One of its main uses is in making fertilizers. The large amount of nitrogen it contains helps to increase crop production. It is also used in refrigeration, and the textile industry uses it in making synthetic fibers such as nylon and rayon. It is used in the manufacture of many other chemicals and plastics.

Making ammonia

Large quantities of ammonia are made by combining hydrogen and nitrogen under pressure and passing them through hot iron oxide. The iron oxide is a CATALYST. It does not take part in the chemical reaction, but its presence causes the reaction to take place more quickly.

The commercial process for making ammonia was discovered by the German chemists Fritz Haber and Karl Bosch. The process, called the Haber-Bosch process, was very important to Germany during World War I because Germany needed large quantities of ammonia to make gunpowder. The diagram shows a modern ammonia-making plant.

See also: ALKALIS, CHEMISTRY, FERTILIZERS, PLASTICS

The diagram on the right shows how ammonia is made in a modern converter—a container that can stand up to very high pressure. The hydrogen and nitrogen gas is piped in at the bottom. It is heated as it goes up and down the pipes before going through the iron oxide catalyst. The hot iron oxide makes the hydrogen and nitrogen combine to make ammonia. Intense heat is given off during the process. This heat is reduced by putting in "quench" at the top. This quench is simply cold gas which passes through perforated tubes to the catalyst.

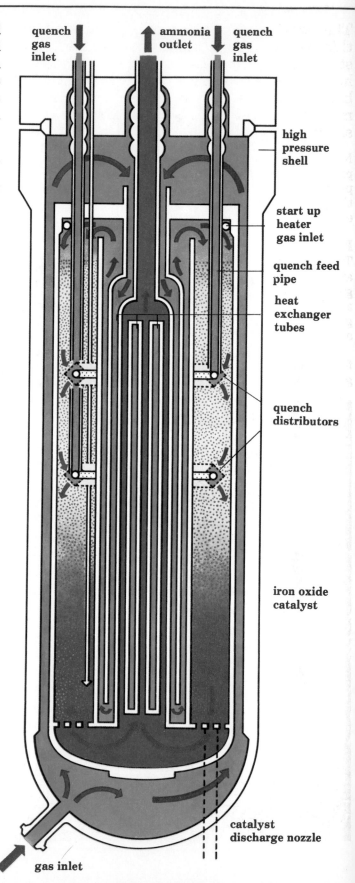

quench gas inlet

ammonia outlet

quench gas inlet

high pressure shell

start up heater gas inlet

quench feed pipe

heat exchanger tubes

quench distributors

iron oxide catalyst

catalyst discharge nozzle

gas inlet

Ammunition

The word ammunition can mean many things—from the small cartridge used in a starter's pistol to the atomic shell fired from a huge cannon. It also includes rifle cartridges, bombs, rockets and torpedoes. The word is most often used to mean gun cartridges and shells.

Nearly all ammunition has three main parts—the projectile (the bullet, shot or warhead that is fired); the propellant (the charge of powder that burns and pushes the projectile out of the gun); and the primer (the high explosive that ignites the propellant powder).

Explosives
There are two main kinds of explosive—high explosive and low explosive. High explosives (such as TNT, gelignite and dynamite) react very fast, usually within a few millionths of a second. The tremendous power given out by this kind of explosion can be used to burst a steel shell into tiny pieces.

Low explosives act much more slowly. They take a few thousandths of a second to react. The pressure given out by low explosives is used in a gun to propel the shell. Explosives have to be compressed (squeezed tightly) in a shell or some other kind of base before they can be set off. If they are not on fire in the open air they usually just burn and do not explode.

Small arms ammunition
Rifle and pistol cartridges are complete units. Each cartridge includes the bullet (the projectile), the powder and the primer. The bullet, usually made of lead alloy, is fitted into the neck of a brass cartridge case. The propellant powder fills the body of the case, while the primer is in the bottom of the case—the part that is struck by the firing pin when the trigger is pulled. When the firing pin strikes the high explosive primer,

Below left: Checking shells during World War I. The shells had steel or cast-iron bodies, and were filled with low-explosive gunpowder or with a high-explosive such as TNT. Shrapnel shells contained small steel balls which shot out in all directions when the shell exploded.

Below: Shells used by NATO soldiers in Germany today. They are 6-inch (155 mm) shells and have a firing range of over 9 miles (14.5 km).

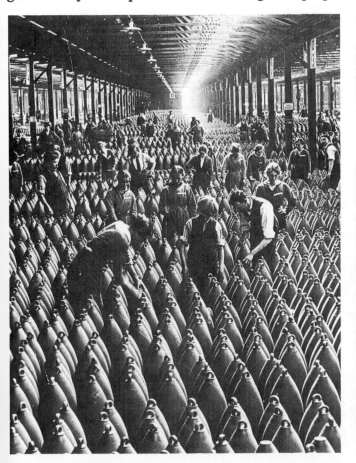

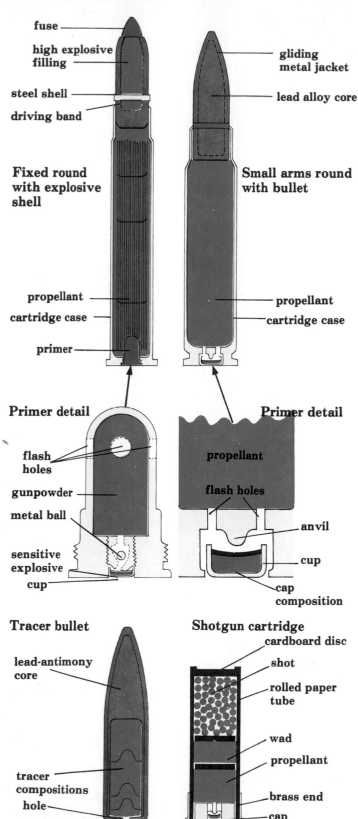

fuse

high explosive filling

steel shell

driving band

gliding metal jacket

lead alloy core

Fixed round with explosive shell

Small arms round with bullet

propellant

cartridge case

primer

propellant

cartridge case

Primer detail

Primer detail

flash holes

gunpowder

metal ball

sensitive explosive cup

propellant

flash holes

anvil

cup

cap composition

Tracer bullet

Shotgun cartridge

lead-antimony core

cardboard disc

shot

rolled paper tube

wad

propellant

brass end

cap

tracer compositions hole

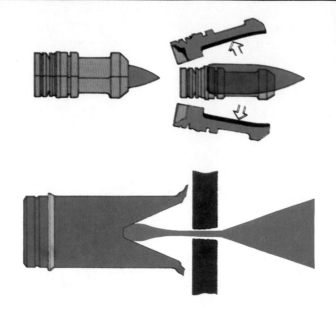

Above: At the top is an armor-piercing shell. As the shell is on its way, the case separates, leaving the very hard tungsten projectile to pierce the enemy armor. The inside of this shell can be seen at the left on the facing page. Below this is a high-explosive antitank shell. As it hits its target, a jet of molten metal and gas is shot through the armor of the tank. A diagram of this can be seen second from left on the facing page.

the primer explodes and sends a flame into the main powder charge. The low explosive powder burns and makes expanding gases which push the bullet out of the barrel at very high speed.

Shotgun ammunition is different. It has a case made of heavy paper. This holds the powder and a number of small lead balls (shot). When the gun is fired, the balls fly from the muzzle and spread out over a wide area.

Shells

Larger shells work in very much the same way as small arms bullets. Shells have a ring of softer material near the bottom. This is called the driving band or rotating band and is made of soft copper, mild steel or plastic. The band is slightly wider than the rest of the shell.

Left top: A high-explosive shell, and beside it a diagram of a small arms bullet. Below these are details showing how the primers work. The gun's firing pin strikes the cap, setting off the high-explosive in the primer. This small explosion ignites the propellant, pushing the shell or bullet out of the gun. At bottom left is a tracer bullet, and beside it a shotgun cartridge holding lead shot.

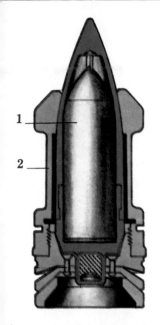
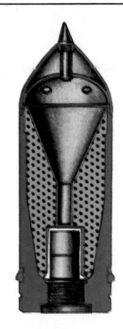

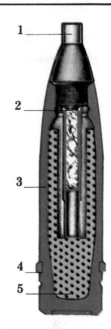

An armor-piercing anti-tank shell. It has a projectile made of very hard tungsten carbide (1), surrounded by a light alloy sleeve (2).

A high-explosive antitank shell. On the facing page you can see how it shoots molten metal through the enemy armor.

Another high-explosive antitank shell. This shell has a soft nose (1) and is filled with a large amount of plastic high-explosive (2).

A high-explosive shell, showing nose cap (1), fuse assembly (2), outer casing (3), driving band (4), and the high-explosive filling (5).

When the gun is fired, the band digs into a spiral groove cut into the inside of the gun barrel. This makes the shell spin and fly much straighter than it would if there were no rifling in the gun.

Bullets for small weapons have a softer metal jacket which works in the same way as a rotating band. The jacket digs into the groove inside the barrel and makes the bullet spin.

Shells that have explosive in them carry some kind of fuse to explode the filling. Most fuses are made to explode the shell as soon as it touches its target, or a fraction of a second later. Some armor-piercing shells have a fuse which goes off only after the shell has gone through the metal of the target. All fuses are very complicated; they have to be designed not to go off during the firing of the gun, when they come under enormous pressure. However, they must still go off when they hit the target.

Other kinds of ammunition

Tracer bullets are filled with material that burns in flight so that the person firing the bullets can see whether they are hitting their target. They are used in machine gun ammunition belts along with ordinary bullets to improve aiming.

During World War II, a new type of weapon was used—the bazooka antitank weapon. The bazooka was fired from the shoulder, and its ammunition was a rocket filled with high explosive.

New ammunition

In recent years, cartridges have been tried which have two or three bullets inside them, one behind the other. When fired, the bullets spread apart slightly, so one of them has a better chance of hitting the target. Other cartridges contain several thin steel arrows, and are very effective at short range.

In the U.S. a great deal of work is being done to reduce the weight of cartridges and find a material to replace the brass cartridge case. The best solution seems to be a cartridge case which is also the propellant. The bullet is fixed in a solid cylinder of propellant, made like a normal cartridge case. When the rifle is fired, the cartridge case is totally burned up and makes a hot gas which pushes the bullet through the rifle barrel.

Since World War II, rifle bullets have become shorter, lighter and very fast moving. In the future, shells may have liquid propellant instead of the powder now used. They may be fired by electricity rather than today's percussion cap.

See also: ANTIAIRCRAFT GUNS, EXPLOSIVES, GUNS

Amphibious Vehicles

Amphibious vehicles are just as good at traveling on water as on land. In the water they are pushed along by a propeller or jets of water. On land they move on wheels or tracks. They are used by the armed forces for amphibious landings and crossing rivers.

Not much is known about the first amphibious vehicles. In 1805, Oliver Evans, an American engineer, was requested to dredge Philadelphia's docks. He built a steam dredger which was supposed to come ashore and drive from one part of the docks to another. However, his vehicle does not seem to have been very successful.

A century later the Fournier amphibious car was made in France. On land, the engine turned the rear wheels as usual, but in the water it turned a propeller. It was the first amphibious vehicle.

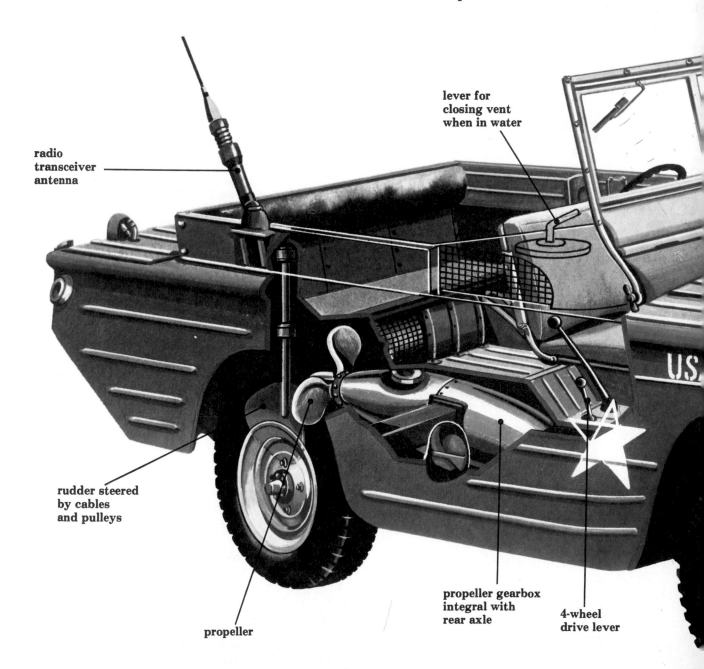

radio transceiver antenna

lever for closing vent when in water

rudder steered by cables and pulleys

propeller

propeller gearbox integral with rear axle

4-wheel drive lever

Military amphibians

It was World War II that saw the introduction of the first military amphibians. In 1942 General Motors began making the Duplex Universal Karrier, Wheeled (DUKW or "Duck"). It was intended mainly as a way of getting men and supplies ashore from ships. It had six wheels, all steerable and all powered by the engine. In the water the wheels helped the rudder to steer.

This remarkable vehicle weighed 6½ tons and could travel at 50 miles per hour (80 kilometers per hour) on land and 6 mph (10 km/h) in water.

General Motors stopped making DUKWs in 1945, but these "go-anywhere" vehicles are still being used by many armies and navies. They were turned out in their thousands during the war and played an important part in the invasion of Europe by the Allies and in the Pacific.

The LVT

The LVT (Landing Vehicle, Tracked) uses a different method. It has tracks like a tank instead of wheels, but the tracks are special ones with pieces sticking out from them like paddles to push the LVT along in the water.

It was developed from a rescue vehicle designed by Donald Roebling called the Buffalo which was used in the swamps of Florida in the 1930s. With its tracks it could travel up rocky beaches or in heavy surf without any trouble.

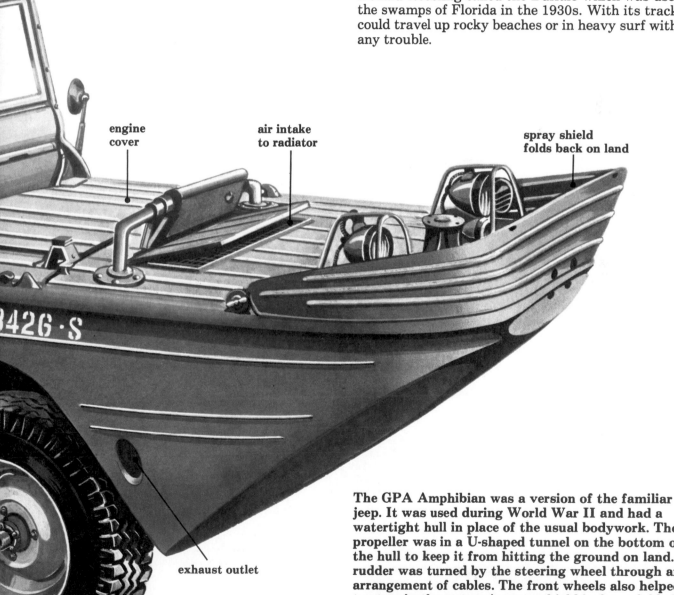

engine
cover

air intake
to radiator

spray shield
folds back on land

3426·S

exhaust outlet

The GPA Amphibian was a version of the familiar jeep. It was used during World War II and had a watertight hull in place of the usual bodywork. The propeller was in a U-shaped tunnel on the bottom of the hull to keep it from hitting the ground on land. A rudder was turned by the steering wheel through an arrangement of cables. The front wheels also helped to steer in the water. A spray shield in front folded back to uncover the lights.

Floating tanks

Tanks, too, were converted to amphibians so that they could get ashore under their own power from ships during a seaborne invasion and, once ashore, could cross rivers. The Sherman tanks took part in the Normandy invasions in June 1944 with a special drive invented by Nicholas Straussler.

At first they were equipped with a propeller turned by a device that took its power from the tracks. But it was found that the propellers were constantly hitting stones and other objects while the tank was ashore. So water jet propulsion was used instead. A propeller in a duct underneath the tank took in water and jetted it out through tubes at the back. These jets pushed the tank along in the water.

Water jet propulsion is now the favorite way of powering amphibious vehicles of all kinds. Modern tanks are lighter than those of the past, and so it is easier to make them float. Some of today's Russian tanks are efficient amphibians. One of the best is the water jet-powered PT-76.

Underwater tanks

Other tanks can go completely underwater to allow them to get close to the enemy without being seen. German tanks of this kind would have been used against Britain in Hitler's planned invasion of England. The Americans, too, had underwater tanks.

Tanks that go right under the water still need air for their engines. The answer was to have a long tube called a snorkel running up from the tank to the surface through which it could get air. (The same method was used by the German U-boats to avoid having to surface completely before using their main diesel engines.)

One of today's tanks that uses a snorkel is France's AMX30. Its 15-foot (4.6-meter) snorkel is big enough for one of the tank crew to get in and put his head out of the top, so that he can make sure they are going in the right direction.

The Austin Champ, a British version of the American jeep, also used a snorkel.

The amphibious jeep

The jeep itself came in an amphibious version, too. It was called the GPA (General Purpose Amphibious). It had a watertight body in place of the usual jeep body, and the propeller was mounted well out of the way under the chassis. Its top speed was 50 mph (80 km/h) on the flat, in spite of having to carry more weight.

The Germans also had an amphibious vehicle called the Volkswagen Schwimmwagen, which they used during World War II.

Pleasure vehicles

People have also had amphibians just for fun. For instance, during the 1960s the Germans built the

Left and below: LVTs coming ashore during operations in the Mediterranean. These vehicles are about 30 ft (10 m) long, 12 ft (4 m) wide and 10 ft (3 m) high. They can carry between 25 and 30 troops and weigh about 38 tons when fully laden.

Amphicar, a rear-engined soft-top. It had twin nylon propellers, and in the water the driver steered it with its front wheels, just as though it were on land. The tires also helped to keep the car afloat.

The British Hydrocar was an amphibian with an unusually high speed. It could go 95 mph (153 km/h) on land and 30 knots (56 km/h) in the water. All four wheels were driven by the engine on land, but retracted into the body once it was in the water. Afloat it was powered by a large water jet.

The ATVs

Most of today's amphibious vehicles are called ATVs (All Terrain Vehicles, meaning that they can go on any kind of surface). They have big soft tires that are hardly inflated at all, and most have six or eight wheels. This shares the weight of the vehicle over a large area of tire tread, to give enormous grip and prevent the ATV sinking into soft ground.

ATVs are steered like a tank. To make it turn to the left, the wheels (or the track on a tank) on the right-hand side are made to go around faster than those on the left-hand side. The wheels are also used to propel the ATV in the water.

The swamp buggy

The swamp buggy was specially developed for getting around in the marshy land of the Everglades in Florida.

It is an amphibian that has huge tires, often taken from earthmoving equipment or from airplanes, to take it safely through water and boggy ground.

In New Zealand they tried a different idea. It was simply a specially made raft which supported the vehicle in the water. The raft had rollers at the back connected to a propeller. The truck or car was driven onto the raft, and the back wheels were placed on the rollers, so that they could turn the propeller. The front wheels went through holes into the water, and the driver used them to steer the raft.

The air-cushion vehicle

Air-cushion vehicles that float on a cushion of air underneath the hull are more efficient than the amphibians and are taking over from them. Nearly all amphibians have to stop to change over from land to water use. Air-cushion vehicles can just sail on from dry or swampy land to sea without a pause.

Nowadays people are using pleasure amphibians more and more, and many of them are being constructed by do-it-yourself enthusiasts.

See also: AIR-CUSHION VEHICLES, HYDROFOIL, INTERNAL COMBUSTION ENGINE, PROPELLER, TANKS

Anchors

The word anchor comes from the Greek word for hook, and anchors are really just large hooks which catch onto the seabed to hold a ship in place. The weight of the heavy anchor chain lying on the bottom also helps to hold large ships.

Most anchors are shaped so that a pull sideways makes them dig firmly into the seabed, but an upward pull releases the anchor easily. It is attached to the ship by a cable—a heavy chain in large ships. Anchor chains are made of special high-grade steel. The cable must be flat for some distance along the seabed if the anchor is to do its job properly. The length of cable paid out from the ship should be from three to eight times the depth of water. The usefulness of an anchor also depends a great deal on the kind of seabed it lands on.

To weigh anchor means to pull the anchor up from the bottom. This is done by a machine called a WINCH which hauls in the cable until the ship is right over the anchor. When the cable is vertical, the anchor comes away from the seabed easily.

Early anchors
The earliest anchors were stone weights. Many ancient anchors have been found in the Mediterranean Sea, some dating back to the Bronze Age. Some time after 1000 BC, metal began to be used. Huge wooden anchors had lead stocks (crosspieces at the top). The stock was at right angles to the arms that carried the flukes (the points that dig into the sea bottom). If the stock touched the bottom first, the anchor twisted over so that a fluke stuck in instead.

By the time of Christ, the traditional fixed anchor came into use. You can see one on the left of the illustration below. This type of anchor was used until well into the 19th century.

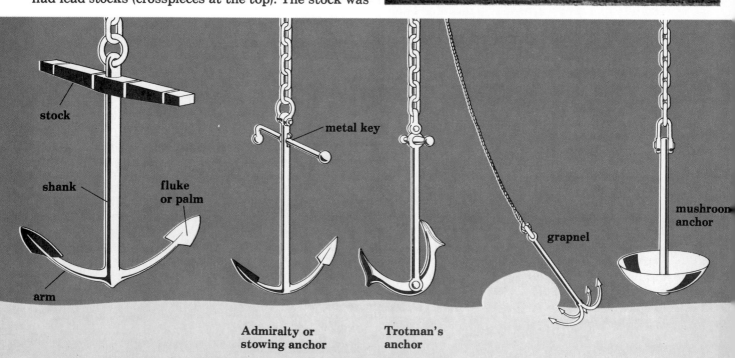

stock

shank

fluke or palm

arm

metal key

Admiralty or stowing anchor

Trotman's anchor

grapnel

mushroom anchor

Today's anchors

Large fixed anchors were rather difficult to handle, so a kind that could be stowed more easily was invented. This was the Admiralty or stowing anchor. Its stock had one bent end and was held in place by a metal key when in use. But the stock could be folded along the length of the anchor for stowing. This anchor can be found in yachts and other small craft.

Trotman's anchor has a pivoted fluke to help it dig into the sea bottom.

Stockless anchors

The anchor used in most modern ships is the stockless anchor. Its large flukes are pivoted and it has tripping

Left: This mosaic, made of thousands of small pieces of different-colored stone, was found at Dougga in Tunisia. It was made by an ancient Roman and shows a man carrying an anchor. The anchor is of the stockless kind, and would have been very difficult to secure.

Below: Some of the main kinds of anchor. At the right is the stockless anchor. When it is lowered, the flukes fall to one side as shown by the dotted lines. When a tripping palm touches the seabed, the flukes turn as shown in the first side view. Then, as the drag becomes more sideways, the flukes begin to dig in. The traditional fixed anchor is shown on the left.

palms that make sure the flukes stick into the seabed. Since this anchor has no stock, it can be pulled right up to the opening in the bow (front) of the ship called the hawespipe. Most large ships carry two anchors.

The Danforth anchor uses a small stock at the bottom to help it dig in. The CQR or plow anchor has a single fluke shaped like a plowshare which digs itself deeper the more it is pulled.

Grapnel anchors are used by small craft. Mushroom anchors are mostly used to moor lightships and dredgers permanently to a soft seabed. After a while, the mushroom sinks deeply and is held in place by suction.

Sea anchors

A sea anchor is a device shaped like a large sock which floats on the water and is let out over the bows of boats in heavy weather. Its drag brings the craft around so that it always faces in the direction of the wind.

The drogue is a sea anchor used by small boats when landing through a surf to prevent the boat being thrown broadside to the sea.

The kedge is a small anchor used to move a ship short distances by carrying the anchor out in a boat, letting it go and then hauling the ship up to it. It may also be used to change the direction in which is heading by moving the bow or stern around.

See also: SHIP BUILDING

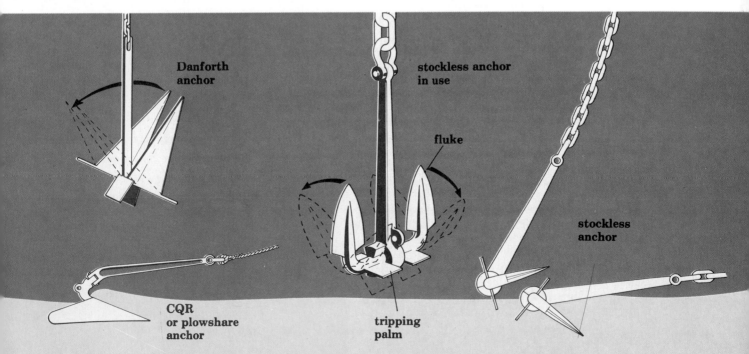

Danforth anchor

stockless anchor in use

fluke

CQR or plowshare anchor

tripping palm

stockless anchor

Anesthetics

Drugs called anesthetics are among the miracles of modern medicine. They make it possible for operations and other medical treatments to be carried out painlessly. A local anesthetic produces numbness in one part of the body while the patient remains awake. A general anesthetic makes the patient unconscious.

Before anesthetics were used, even the most minor operation could be very painful. You have only to look at early drawings of people having teeth pulled to realize how lucky we are today. Modern anesthetics fall into several groups according to how and where they act to reduce pain. They can be given to patients in various ways.

General anesthetics
These can be given either by injection or as a gas to breathe in (inhale). The injection is termed intravenous, which means that it is made into a vein. Usually, the injection is given in the arm or in the back of the hand. The gas enters the body through a mask that covers the nose and mouth. Sometimes, a patient given an injection of anesthetic is given gas later to keep him or her unconscious for longer.

General anesthetics should always be given by a trained anesthetist—a medical doctor trained in the use of anesthetics. The anesthetist controls how much anesthetic is given to the patient during the operation. The patient's condition is checked all the time so that immediate action can be taken if there are any signs of trouble.

To the patient, loss of consciousness may seem to occur quickly. It is actually a gradual process that happens in three different stages. At first, the patient feels drowsy, but may become restless and talk aloud. This is called the induction stage. During the second stage, the patient is unconscious. The breathing is irregular, and the muscles may still respond when tapped. In the third stage, the patient is fully unconscious, with regular breathing and relaxed muscles.

In recent years, many new anesthetic gases have been developed. All have a pleasant odor and ensure a quick return to consciousness after the operation.

Before being given a general anesthetic, patients are usually injected with a mixture of drugs called premedication. This causes drowsiness and helps to relax the muscles. By preparing a patient in this way, the job of the anesthetist is made much easier.

Local anesthetics
The most common way of giving a local anesthetic is by injection. Dentists often inject the patient's mouth with a local anesthetic. This deadens the nerves in the area so that pain signals do not reach the brain. Teeth can then be pulled or drilled without hurting the patient. Some local anesthetics come in the form of an ointment, which is rubbed on the affected area. Another type is applied as a spray. And, if an internal area is to be treated, a jelly-like anesthetic can be swallowed.

The great advantage of giving a local anesthetic instead of a general anesthetic is that the patient remains conscious. He or she can then cooperate with the doctor or surgeon to make the operation easier.

Controlling anesthesia
Anesthesia—the patient's loss of feeling—must be controlled carefully. Too much anesthetic could be dangerous. Too little could mean that the patient will

Below: Sir Humphry Davy's gas machine of 1800. Davy was one of the first to experiment with nitrous oxide (laughing gas) as an anesthetic.

Bottom: An operation at the Royal Hospital, Belfast, in 1885 using ether. Ether was probably the first anesthetic in surgery.

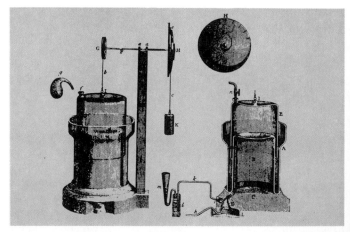

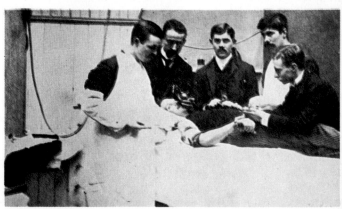

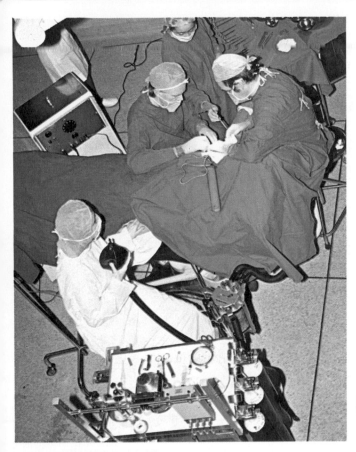

Above: An anesthetic machine in an operating room, showing pipelines and cylinders.

Right: Two types of anesthetic apparatus. Above is the open-circuit system, and below is the closed-circuit system.

Anesthetic machines

A common type of anesthetic machine is known as Boyle's apparatus. It was introduced in 1917, but has been much improved since then. The equipment usually rests on a movable trolley, or is installed close to the operating table. Gas may be supplied from cylinders attached to the machine. It may also be piped from a central supply in another part of the hospital. In this case, the machine may have cylinders of gas for use only if the main supply should fail.

Color codes

The cylinders are color coded for easy identification. Usually, there are two oxygen cylinders (black with white tops), two of nitrous oxide (blue), one of carbon dioxide (gray), and one small cylinder of cyclopropane (orange). Carbon dioxide helps to stimulate breathing, should this become weak.

Each gas supply has a different kind of connector. This is a safety measure so that the inlets on the machine cannot be connected to the wrong supplies by mistake. Cyclopropane is supplied at low pressure and can be fed directly into the machine. The other gases

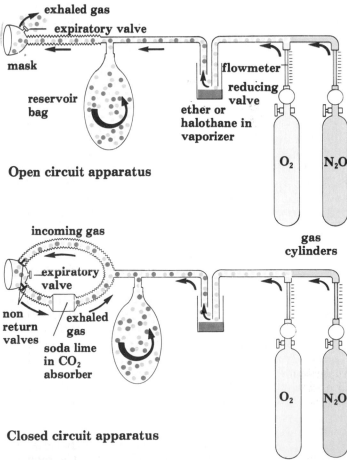

feel pain. During a simple operation using a local anesthetic, a measured quantity of known strength is usually injected at the start. Normally, the operation is completed long before the numbness wears off. In longer operations, such as childbirth, doses of local anesthetic may be given at intervals through a needle left in the patient. For long-lasting action, an anesthetic called bupivacaine is used. But the drug most widely used for local anesthetics is lignocaine.

General anesthetics given by injection are controlled in a similar way to local anesthetic injections. However, when gas is used for a general anesthetic, a more elaborate means of control is required. Besides inhaling the anesthetic, the patient must take in air or oxygen to breathe. And he must be able to exhale too. All these processes are carried out through an anesthetic machine.

The type of machine used depends on the kind of operation being carried out, and on the anesthetic used.

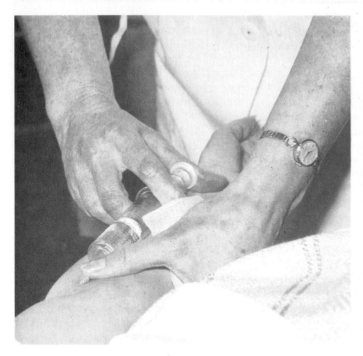

Above: An injection of general anesthetic is given in a vein in the arm. It is sometimes injected into the back of the hand.

Right: After taking the patient from the ward, he or she is given oxygen before being injected with a general anesthetic.

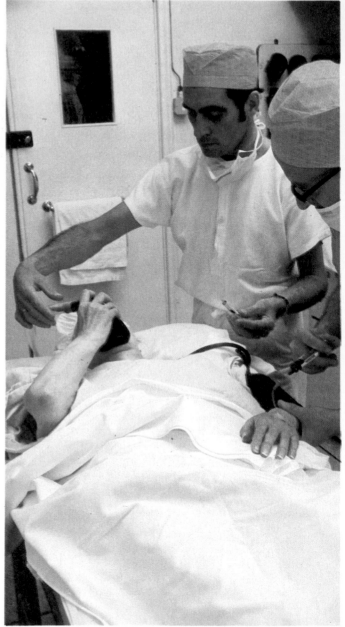

are stored at high pressure. A suitably low pressure is obtained by passing each of these gases through a device called a reducing valve.

The anesthetist decides on a suitable mixture of gases to use. This is determined by the degree of unconsciousness required, the patient's health and age, and the type of surgery being performed. Each of the chosen gases is passed through a flowmeter. This is a tapered vertical tube containing a loosely fitting plunger. The gas flows around the plunger, forcing it up the tube. The rate of gas flow is indicated by the height at which the plunger hovers. A rapid flow is required to keep it at the top, where the tube is widest. The tube is made of transparent material so that the position of the plunger can be seen. A scale beside the tube shows the corresponding gas flow rate.

Vapor from liquid anesthetics is sometimes added to the gas mixture. To do this, the gases are passed over or through the liquid in a container called a vaporizer. Some of the liquid EVAPORATES and is carried along by the gas stream. The mixture passes into a rubber reservoir bag. When the patient breathes in (inhales) through his face mask, he partially empties this bag. It is refilled while the patient breathes out (exhales).

The exhaled gases leave the mask through a valve, so that waste carbon dioxide gas cannot build up and cause suffocation. To reduce the risk of explosion, the flammable gas mixture exhaled is often carried away through tubes. Systems in which the exhaled gases leave the apparatus are called open-circuit systems.

In closed-circuit systems, the exhaled gases are passed through a cylinder containing a chemical mixture called soda-lime. This absorbs the carbon dioxide, so that the remaining gases can be re-used. Much simpler machines are used in dental surgeries, where a mixture of nitrous oxide and oxygen is used.

TYPES OF ANESTHETIC

Anesthetic	Effect	How given	Time needed to act
General	Complete loss of consciousness.	Two methods: *Intravenous*—injection through a vein, usually at elbow or in hand (for shorter surgical or dental operations). *Inhalation*—given as gas through a mask (for longer operations or to maintain intravenous anesthesia).	Rapid loss of consciousness. If patients told to count to 10—usually "out" by the time they reach number 7.
Local	"Freezing" or numbing of particular area, e.g. gum and teeth in dentistry.	Applied by spray or swab. Made up in solution for injection or as drops. As a gel or ointment.	On surface—almost immediately. Under skin—within minutes.
Spinal (An epidural)	Gives pain relief without loss of consciousness—for childbirth, gynecological or spinal operations.	Injected into epidural layer of spinal canal.	In minutes.
Obstetric	Pain relief in childbirth without loss of consciousness. Slight drowsiness.	Inhaled through mask held in hand. Automatically dropped when too drowsy.	Only momentary loss of consciousness.

STAGES OF GENERAL ANESTHESIA

Pre-medication	Stage One	Stage Two	Stage Three
A sedative injection is given to calm and relax patient while still in hospital ward. Can be combined with muscle relaxant injection.	Pleasant sleep-like effect. Loss of consciousness begins. Some restlessness and talking aloud. (Stage One is reached with gas and air pain relief in childbirth).	Patient is unconscious but reflexes still present. Breathing not quite regular.	Patient is fully unconscious. Breathing is quiet and regular. Muscles relaxed.

Pain relief in childbirth

For normal childbirth, the woman needs to be conscious. So, to relieve any pain, a local anesthetic called an epidural may be given. This is injected into the spine and repeated when necessary. It stops pain signals being sent via the spinal cord to the brain.

Another technique allows the woman to breathe in a mixture of nitrous oxide and oxygen through a mask. She holds the mask in her hand. If she becomes too drowsy, she will drop the mask and start breathing air again. In this way, she can have pain relief without completely losing consciousness.

After-effects

Modern anesthetics produce few after-effects. With local and spinal anesthetics, the numbness may take a few hours to wear off. Sometimes the site of the injection may ache slightly for a short time. Sickness, once common after having a general anesthetic, is now rare. A drowsy feeling may persist, so it is safer to have someone drive the patient back home after their operation.

See also: BACTERIA, BRAIN, DENTISTRY, SURGERY

Antennas

Antennas, or aerials, are used for sending (transmitting) or receiving radio waves. They are used in radio, television and radar systems. Astronomers use large antennas to pick up the radio waves from remote and distant galaxies.

Transmission and reception
To transmit (send) radio signals, an antenna changes electrical signals from a transmitter into radio waves. These waves spread out from the antenna and can travel through the air and through space. They travel at the speed of light.

When the radio waves reach a receiving antenna, they are changed back into electrical signals. These can be strengthened (amplified) in a receiver, which then takes useful information from the signals. In the case of a radio broadcast, for example, the transmitted radio waves carry sound signals. In the receiver, the sound signals are taken from the radio signals and will be reproduced through a loudspeaker.

A radio transmitter produces a signal in the form of an alternating current. This means that the current moves to and fro—or oscillates. The rate at which this happens is called the frequency of the transmission, and is measured in kilohertz (kHz) or megahertz (MHz). One kilohertz is a frequency of 1000 cycles (oscillations) per second. It is sometimes called one kilocycle (kc/s). One megahertz is a frequency of 1,000,000 cycles per second, or megacycle per second (Mc/s).

The alternating current flowing in the transmitting antenna produces radio waves around it. These spread out from the antenna like ripples in a pond. When the radio waves reach a receiving antenna, they cause a small current to flow in the antenna. This current alternates, like the one in the transmitting antenna. Signals from other transmitters will reach the receiving antenna too. These will have different frequencies. A circuit in the receiver allows signals of only one particular frequency to be selected, or tuned.

Radio stations
When there were few radio stations, the tuning dials often used to show the names of stations that could be received. Today, however, there are so many stations that their names would not all fit on the dial. Modern sets usually just show the frequencies to which that radio can be tuned. Sometimes the tuning scale will show the wavelength too. This is simply the length of one complete radio wave, and is normally given in meters.

Left: The huge dish of this radio telescope focuses radio signals onto the small antenna at its center. With this equipment, extremely weak signals from outer space can be picked up. The dish can be steered to cover most of the sky. Radio astronomers learn much about the universe from the signals sent out by various stars and heavenly bodies. Many of these objects cannot be seen through optical telescopes. Radio observations provide the only proof of their existence. In other cases, radio observations add to the information obtained by visual study.

Wavelength and frequency

The relationship between wavelength and frequency is important in radio engineering. It is the frequency that determines the wavelength of the signals. The wavelength determines the ideal sizes of the transmitting and receiving antennas. In general, the longer the wavelength, the larger the antennas needed for it to work efficiently.

Radio signals move at a fixed speed of 300 million meters per second. So, however many waves are produced in one second, they will occupy a distance of 300 million meters. If, for example, there are 300 million waves, then each wave will be exactly 1 meter long. So we can say that a frequency of 300 million waves per second (MHz) makes a wavelength of 1 meter. As frequency decreases, so wavelength increases. For example, a frequency of 3 MHz makes a wavelength of 100 meters.

Left: A television transmitting mast carrying microwave "horn" antennas too. The television antenna is at the top of the mast. The rest is a supporting structure. The horn antennas are part of a local communications system.

Antenna design

The design of both transmitting and receiving antennas is very similar. However, a transmitting antenna must be able to handle the high power produced by the transmitter. And, to avoid wasting this power, the antenna is usually carefully designed, adjusted and maintained. For receivers, most people make do with a simple antenna.

The simplest form of antenna is a single wire suspended in the air. Radio engineers call this a MONOPOLE. Long wire antennas can be used for medium frequency radio transmission and reception. Antennas used for very high frequency (VHF) signals are relatively small. They often consist of a DIPOLE—two rods set end to end, with a small gap between them. Many television systems operate in the ultra high frequency (UHF) bands. At such frequencies, efficient antennas can be made quite small. This is why good reception can often be obtained using a small antenna (rabbit ears) on top of the set.

Reflectors

To improve the signal strength sent out or received, some antennas are often fitted with reflectors. These often consist of a simple metal element, placed to one side of the main part of the antenna. Besides a reflector, rooftop television antennas normally have a series of directors to further increase the signal strength.

Antennas used for radio astronomy and radar use parabolic (dish-shaped) reflectors to increase signal strength.

See also: ASTRONOMY, RADIO,
RADIO TELESCOPE, TELEVISION

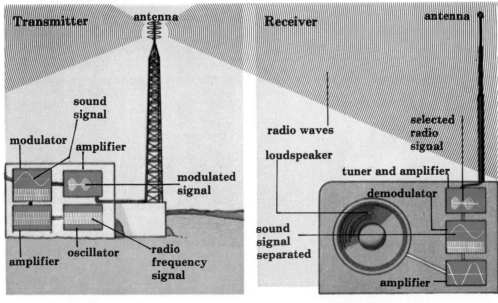

Left: A radio transmitter beams a signal from an antenna on a higher tower. The signal is picked up on the whip antenna of a portable radio receiver. In the transmitter, an oscillator produces a radio-frequency signal. This is strengthened, and a sound signal superimposed on it. The modulated signal is amplified and then sent out. The receiver tunes in the radio waves, and separates the sound signal for reproduction on a loudspeaker.

Antiaircraft Guns

Antiaircraft guns were first used in World War I when airplanes were being used for military purposes. They were even more important in World War II, but today, long-range antiaircraft guns are no longer used. Jet aircraft fly too high and too fast for ordinary guns to be able to hit them.

The main function of the antiaircraft gun in modern warfare is to stop enemy aircraft flying low enough to observe, photograph, bomb with accuracy or attack troops.

The problems of antiaircraft gunnery

While an antiaircraft (AA) shell is traveling upward toward its target, the target itself is moving through the sky. For example, an airplane traveling at only 200 mph (320 km/h) would travel almost 1¾ miles (2.8 kilometers) during the 30 seconds it could take a shell to reach it. The gunners know the position of the aircraft at the moment the shell is fired. Once the shell is in flight, however, nothing can be done to control it. The gunner has to guess what the plane will do during the flight of the shell. It has to be assumed that the plane will stay on a steady course, and that it will keep to a certain height and speed. Of course, the higher and faster the airplane is flying, the longer the time of flight of the shell, and the more difficult it is to judge any of these movements.

An apparatus to pinpoint the future position of aircraft was developed. It was called the predictor. The predictor followed the path of the plane and measured its bearing (direction) and elevation. The change in bearing and elevation in a short time allowed the course and speed of the plane to be worked out. A range finder was used to give the height of the aircraft. This gave all the information needed by the AA gunners. In the early guidance systems, optical range finders were used, but these were no good at night and were replaced by radar. The predictor was also fed with information about such things as the speed of the shell as it left the gun, its weight and the weather conditions.

A direct hit from an antiaircraft shell was very

Below: One of the earliest kinds of antiaircraft guns, a machine gun mounted on a wooden post. This one is at an airfield in Germany during World War I.

unlikely. So the shells were given a high-explosive filling which was set off by a time fuse. The time fuse was set automatically to go off at the same time it had been worked out that the shell would reach its target. When the shell exploded, it showered out fragments which covered quite a wide area.

A later type of fuse is called the proximity fuse. This works by using a radio device in the shell itself. When the shell reaches its target, the strength of the radio signal tells the fuse to explode the shell. This device means there is no need to set the fuse before it is fired from the gun.

Types of AA gun

During World War II, two main kinds of antiaircraft gun were developed. One was for defense against attack from low-flying aircraft. The other was to try and bring down medium- and high-flying airplanes.

The light AA guns could be moved around easily, and they had to be aimed and fired very quickly because of the speed at which low-flying planes crossed overhead. These guns were mostly 20 mm or 40 mm weapons. The 20 mm guns were used alone, in pairs or mounted in fours. They fired fused high-explosive shells at the rate of 500 to 700 rounds per minute. These guns were

Above: An automatic 40 mm antiaircraft gun being used by the U.S. Navy. It can fire 160 rounds per minute over a range of 11,000 yards (10,000 meters).

aimed by hand and engaged targets flying up to 400 mph (640 km/h) at ranges of 1000 yards (900 meters) or less.

The 40 mm guns had more high-explosive powder in their shells. They usually fired at about 120 rounds per minute at targets up to 500 feet (150 meters). Although most of the guns had simple, open sights, predictors were sometimes used to work out the position of the enemy aircraft.

The heavy guns

The long-range heavy antiaircraft guns varied from 3-inch caliber (the width of the barrel) up to 5.25-inch. They could be used against aircraft flying at up to 60,000 feet (18,300 meters). Because of the great height and speed of the targets, the control equipment was complicated. The need to fire large shells meant that they had to be loaded automatically.

The future of the AA gun

The invention of the jet engine meant that planes could

fly much higher and faster. So the heavy AA gun is no longer used by modern forces. The chance of a hit is too small. These weapons have been replaced by ground-to-air missiles which can change course in flight. They can also fly to great heights and seek out and destroy the enemy plane before it can reach its target.

The use of very high speed fighter-bombers flying at low ALTITUDE has meant that the lighter AA guns still have an important role to play. These weapons have very rapid fire rates. They also have very complicated control gear, often linked to early warning radars.

See also: AMMUNITION, GUNS, MISSILES, RADAR

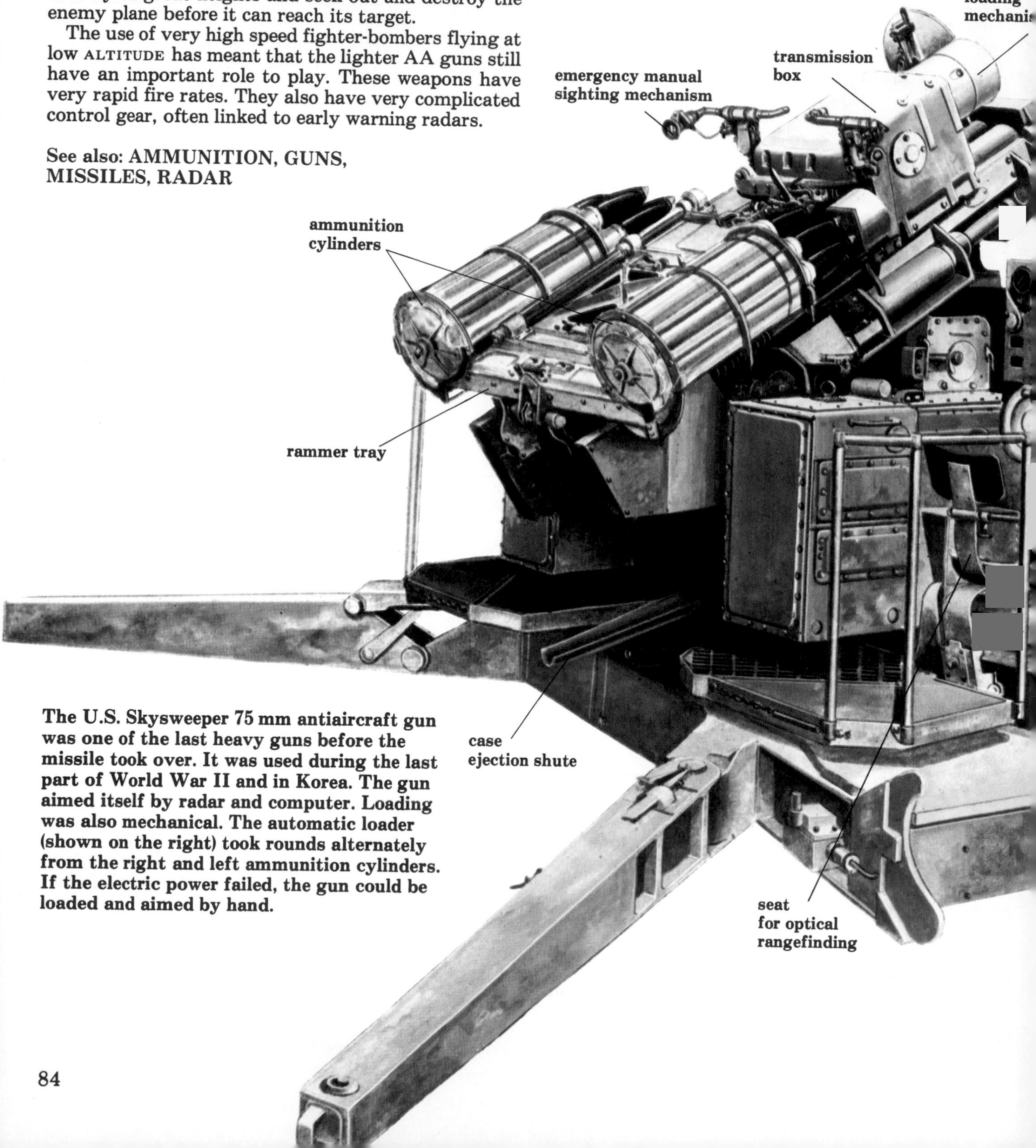

motor to drive loading mechani

transmission box

emergency manual sighting mechanism

ammunition cylinders

rammer tray

The U.S. Skysweeper 75 mm antiaircraft gun was one of the last heavy guns before the missile took over. It was used during the last part of World War II and in Korea. The gun aimed itself by radar and computer. Loading was also mechanical. The automatic loader (shown on the right) took rounds alternately from the right and left ammunition cylinders. If the electric power failed, the gun could be loaded and aimed by hand.

case ejection shute

seat for optical rangefinding

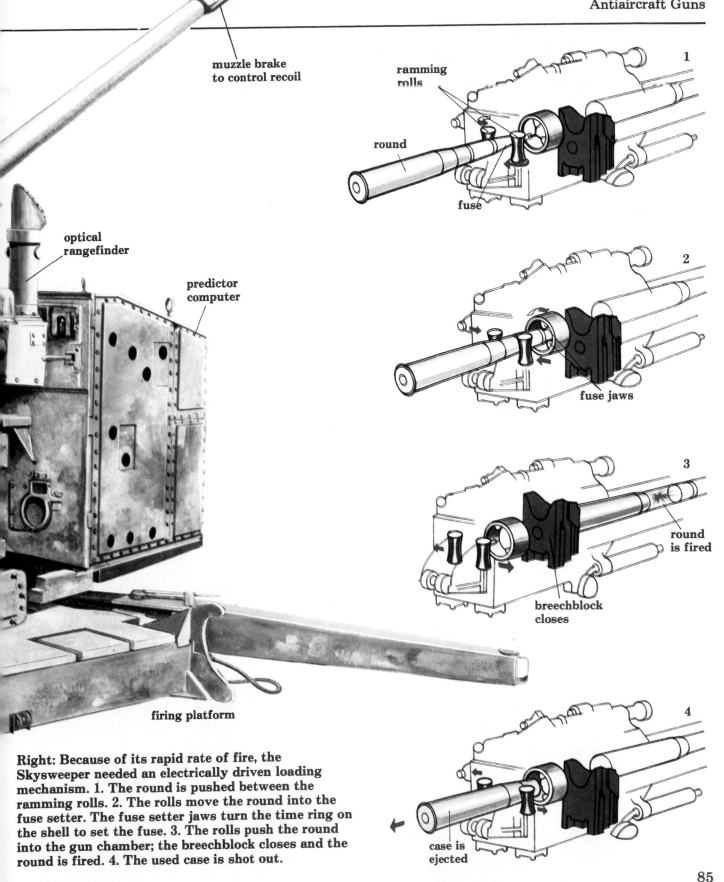

muzzle brake
to control recoil

ramming
rolls

round

fuse

optical
rangefinder

predictor
computer

fuse jaws

round
is fired

breechblock
closes

firing platform

case is
ejected

Right: Because of its rapid rate of fire, the Skysweeper needed an electrically driven loading mechanism. 1. The round is pushed between the ramming rolls. 2. The rolls move the round into the fuse setter. The fuse setter jaws turn the time ring on the shell to set the fuse. 3. The rolls push the round into the gun chamber; the breechblock closes and the round is fired. 4. The used case is shot out.

Antibiotics

True antibiotics are drugs produced from tiny life forms called microorganisms. These include bacteria and fungi. Similar drugs, made by chemical means, are called antibiotics, too. Both types are extremely important for fighting disease in humans, animals and plants.

The great discovery

The first antibiotic was discovered by accident in 1928. Sir Alexander Fleming was studying the bacteria that cause boils and blood poisoning. One day, he noticed that some dishes containing the bacteria had become infected with a mold (a form of fungus). Around the mold, all the bacteria had been killed. The mold was *Penicillium notatum*, and Fleming found that it could kill other harmful bacteria too.

Penicillin production

Many simple organisms float around in the air and reproduce when they settle in suitable conditions. Diseases are often caused in this way. This is how the disease-fighting mold infected Fleming's dishes. Although Fleming was able to grow more of the mold, it proved extremely difficult to make large quantities of the antibiotic it produced. The problem of penicillin production was eventually solved by Howard Florey and Ernst Chain. Large-scale production started when it was necessary to cope with war casualties. For their work with penicillin, Fleming, Florey and Chain received the Nobel Prize for medicine in 1945.

Since the discovery of penicillin, hundreds of other antibiotics have been found. Some are unsuitable for medical use. Others, such as tetracycline and streptomycin, have proved to be of great value in fighting disease.

Antibiotics in action

Antibiotics work in various ways against the micro-organisms that cause disease. Penicillin and related antibiotics are extremely effective against many types of bacteria. Tetracycline is another antibiotic that can be used for a wide range of bacterial infections. Other antibiotics work against a much smaller range of micro-organisms. Different antibiotics of this kind are often combined for effective treatment.

Most types of antibiotics are used to fight the bacteria that cause diseases in man and animals. Other antibiotics fight diseases caused by microscopic fungi. Infections of this kind occur in both animals and plants.

In humans, various types of penicillin are used to treat tonsillitis, pneumonia, meningitis, bronchitis and urinary infections. Penicillin is the most widely used antibiotic. Some forms are usually given by injection.

Others are available in the form of pills and capsules.

The antibiotic tetracycline is used to fight infection of the urinary and respiratory (breathing) systems, and some forms of serious bone infection. It is also used

Above: Two antibiotic crystallization units in operation. Solutions of the antibiotics are filtered and then piped to the crystallizers. Before a batch of material is processed, the whole system is sterilized.

Left: A colony of the green mold *Penicillium chrysogenum*. Most commercial penicillin is produced from this mold.

against the skin disease called acne. Tetracycline is usually taken by mouth.

Other common antibiotics include erythromycin, ampicillin and a more recently developed group called cephalosporins. These were developed from microorganisms discovered in sewage on the Mediterranean island of Sardinia. In addition to the antibiotics mentioned here, there are many others.

Like humans, animals respond well to antibiotic treatment to combat disease. Livestock are also given antibiotics to increase their growth. In this case small amounts of the drugs are mixed with the food.

Some antibiotics are used in large quantities to fight fungal diseases in crops. These diseases include the infections known as rusts and smuts. In Japan, 10,000 tons of blasticidin-S are used each year against the serious fungus disease called rice blast.

The bacteria fight back
A few of the bacteria causing a disease may be able to resist the action of an antibiotic. So, after the other bacteria have been killed by the antibiotic, the resistant type may reproduce to form a large COLONY. The disease will then continue, and the original antibiotic will have no further effect. When this happens, a different antibiotic has to be used to fight the disease.

In order to reduce the risk of breeding large quantities of resistant bacteria, the use of antibiotics in humans is carefully controlled. The effect can occur in animals, too, especially those who have regular doses of antibiotics with their food. In many countries, only antibiotics that are not used by humans can be given to animals. This ensures that, if resistant bacteria develop in the animals, human life will not be in danger. For if the bacteria infect a person, they will be fought successfully with antibiotics to which they have never been exposed.

Side effects
Many patients treated with antibiotics suffer from side effects produced by the drugs. Typical side effects include indigestion, diarrhea, deafness and loss of balance. Penicillin causes some people to break out in a rash. Besides being unpleasant, the side effects can sometimes be dangerous.

For this reason, people should be aware of any antibiotics that cause them distress. Their own doctor will keep a record of such details. However, another

The final stages in the production of antibiotics by crystallization. After washing with a solvent, the crystals are directed to a lower level, where they are dried in a vacuum. The man standing is checking the flow of the mixture.

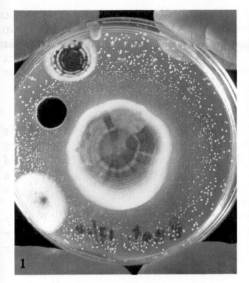

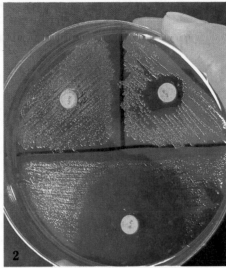

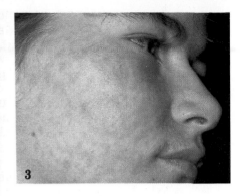

Left and above: Penicillin mold grown in a dish (1) fights three bacteria (2). The dark areas show where the effect is strongest. Rash caused by penicillin (3).

doctor, giving treatment in an emergency, may not have this information. Always inform a new doctor of any antibiotics or other drugs that disagree with you. Never take antibiotics prescribed for someone else.

Production techniques

When penicillin manufacture began in Britain, the only available method was a basic LABORATORY technique. The *Penicillium* mold was grown on the surface of a liquid nutrient—a substance containing chemicals vital to the bacteria's survival. The nutrient was contained in thousands of glass flasks. Once the mold colony had spread to cover the surface of the nutrient, it was removed by pouring the liquid through a filter.

The liquid contained crude penicillin, which had dissolved after being formed in the mold. The penicillin was taken out of the solution, but the amount of the antibiotic obtained in this way was very small. Another problem was that it was often contaminated by substances formed by other microorganisms that had grown on the nutrient.

Deep fermentation

Meanwhile, manufacturers in the United States concentrated on developing improved production methods. They discovered a technique called deep fermentation, which is now used for the production of most antibiotics. Deep fermentation became possible following the discovery of an unusual type of *Penicillium*. This could grow submerged in the nutrient liquid, instead of on the surface. By growing the mold in this way, a given volume of liquid gave a much greater amount of penicillin. Later, other strains of *Penicillium* that gave an even greater amount of the antibiotic were produced. At last, the life-saving drug could be manufactured on a large scale.

Today, master cultures of selected strains of *Penicillium* are stored in controlled conditions. In production, samples of the required culture are taken and allowed to reproduce. Starting from the same source of *Penicillium* each time ensures a consistent quality. The samples, called sub-cultures, are first transferred to culture flasks. There, the mold is grown on a suitable liquid nutrient, and then transferred to a larger vessel. This process is repeated, using larger and larger vessels for the fermentation process.

Final stages

In the final stage, the fermentation tank used may have a capacity of around 30,000 gallons (136,000 liters). In it, the mold grows underwater in a sterilized nutrient broth. This is based on corn-steep liquor, a by-product of the starch industry. To this are added sugar, salts and other chemicals.

The final fermentation lasts from one to two weeks. When it is complete, the contents of the tank are drawn off and filtered to remove the mold. The remaining liquid containing the penicillin is then purified by chemical means and concentrated.

A final chemical process causes the penicillin to appear suddenly as a solid called a PRECIPITATE. The fine crystals formed are filtered out, washed to remove impurities, and then dried and stored. Each batch is carefully tested to make sure that it is active and pure.

By varying the substances in the nutrient broth, various forms of penicillin can be produced. And types that do not occur in nature can be made by chemically treating the pure penicillin.

See also: CHEMISTRY, DRUGS

Aqualung

Divers need air to breathe under water. The air can be pumped down to them through a tube from the surface. But this means they cannot move far from their boat. The aqualung was invented so that divers could take their own air down with them and move about freely.

The aqualung, also called a Self-Contained Underwater Breathing Apparatus (SCUBA), has three main parts.

First there is a cylinder (or sometimes two) with a harness for attaching it to the diver's back. This has the diver's supply of air, pumped into the cylinder under a pressure of about 3000 pounds per square inch (psi). The cylinder is fitted with a pressure gauge so that the diver knows exactly how much air is left.

Secondly the diver has a mouthpiece, like the mouthpiece on a snorkel diving tube. But the aqualung mouthpiece is connected to the cylinder of air by two FLEXIBLE tubes. This is his lifeline to the air supply.

The demand valve

Thirdly he has the most important piece of equipment of all—the demand valve. This is what it is for.

Many people had tried to design an underwater breathing device, but none of them had understood that the air the diver breathed had to be at the same pressure as the water around him. Near the surface the water pressure is much the same as the pressure of the air we breathe all the time. But the water pressure increases as the diver goes down. At quite shallow depths the water pressure outside the diver's body is pushing so hard that he begins to find it difficult to expand his lungs when he breathes. The pressures inside and outside his lungs are not the same.

What he needs is a device for giving him his air supply at exactly the same pressure as the water pressure that surrounds him. In that way the pressures inside and outside his lungs will be equal, and he will be able to breathe without any effort. This is what the demand valve does.

How it works

A simple demand valve is a box with a flexible diaphragm dividing it into two halves. One half is open to the sea. The other half has an inlet from the air cylinder and an outlet to the diver's mouthpiece. The

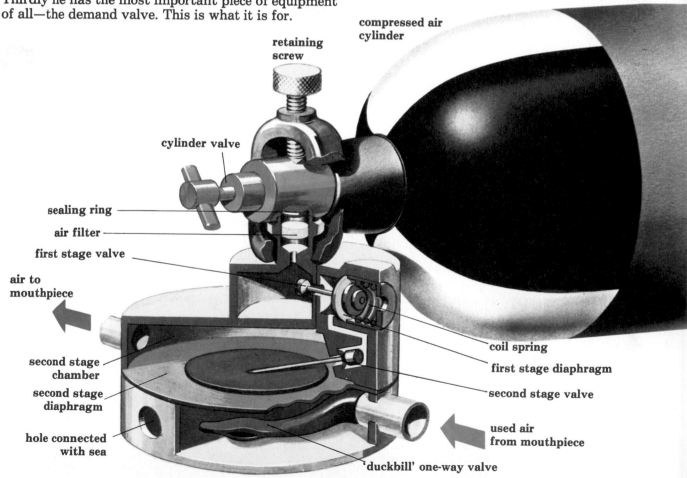

compressed air cylinder

retaining screw

cylinder valve

sealing ring

air filter

first stage valve

air to mouthpiece

second stage chamber

second stage diaphragm

hole connected with sea

coil spring

first stage diaphragm

second stage valve

used air from mouthpiece

'duckbill' one-way valve

inlet from the air cylinder is controlled by a valve which is turned on and off by the diaphragm.

If the water pressure is more than the air pressure, the diaphragm is pushed by the water and the air valve is turned on. The air comes into the air chamber and pushes the diaphragm back against the water pressure until the air pressure and the water pressure are equal. The movement of the diaphragm turns the valve off again, and the air is cut off. So the diver always gets a supply of air at the same pressure as the water around him.

This simple type of demand valve is called single stage. It works well enough at shallow depths, but the water pressure at depth is too great for the single-stage valve to cope with. To stop this problem, the two-stage valve was designed.

In the first stage the air pressure is reduced from the very high pressure of the cylinder to about 100 pounds per square inch above the pressure of the water. This is the first stage. In the second stage this pressure is reduced to water pressure by a valve very like the simple single-stage demand valve.

Using the aqualung

The aqualung diver's stay underwater is limited by the amount of air in the cylinders he carries. However, the long dive times that the aqualung has made possible have been important in underwater archaeology, salvage and rescue operations.

See also: AIR, BATHYSCAPHE, DIVING, SALVAGE, SEA HABITAT, SEA RESCUE, UNDERWATER CAMERA

Above: Aqualung divers usually wear a wet suit. This traps a layer of water between the skin and the material of the suit, and the body heat of the diver soon warms up this trapped water.

Below: The most important part of the diver's equipment is the demand valve. This controls the air supply carried in cylinders on his back so that he is supplied with air at the same pressure as the water around him.

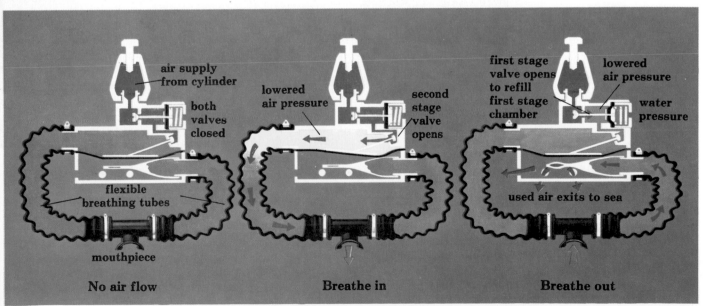

air supply from cylinder

both valves closed

flexible breathing tubes

mouthpiece

No air flow

lowered air pressure

second stage valve opens

Breathe in

first stage valve opens to refill first stage chamber

lowered air pressure

water pressure

used air exits to sea

Breathe out

Archaeological Techniques

Archaeology is becoming more and more scientific. Although the most important work still means careful digging and recording, the archaeologist now relies very much on the scientist to find and date objects left behind by people of long ago.

There are two main parts to all archaeological work. The first is digging (excavating) sites where early people lived. This must be carried out carefully, and every object has to be recorded as it is found. The second part is the study of the objects that are found. Science helps in both these aspects of archaeology.

The clues that help us learn about people of the past and how they lived are the tools, ornaments, buildings and pottery that they left behind. The broken bones of warriors may show what kind of weapons were used. A skeleton may show signs of disease which can be identified by expert examination. The teeth of ancient peoples may tell us something about what they ate. Meat eaters rarely had rotten teeth. The more grain they ate, the more tooth decay can be seen.

Excavating a site
When digging up the past, there is always a risk of destroying valuable evidence. Therefore, good archaeologists work carefully, and note down or photograph everything they find before it is moved.

The director of a dig (the archaeologists' word for "digging" up objects from the past) begins by marking off the site with a surveyor. Then the director selects the areas where the digging will take place. Often it is necessary to explore a site by cutting a trial trench across it. But the best way of digging is to take a square of ground and explore downward within that square. Sometimes a series of squares, with earth walls between them, are dug out to form a grid pattern.

Digging begins with spades and picks. But when undisturbed levels are reached, more delicate tools are needed. Small trowels and brushes are used to gently scrape away the soil around an object. When the object is cleared, it can be sketched or photographed before it is removed to be labeled and recorded.

Preserving valuables
Some of the objects unearthed are so fragile that they rapidly break up when exposed to light, air and damp. Steps must be taken at once to preserve them in coatings of wax or plaster. Objects that were made of wood or cloth generally do not survive, although they sometimes form imprints in the soil. Plaster casts can be made from these imprints, showing the shape of the original object.

Most objects from a site are taken to LABORATORIES for restoration. Broken pieces of pottery are fitted

Left: A dating method in use. An electric current passes between the table legs on one side and spreads through the soil. The voltage is measured between the other two legs. The table is moved around and the readings are fed to a computer. The computer produces a map like the one below of a Roman villa.

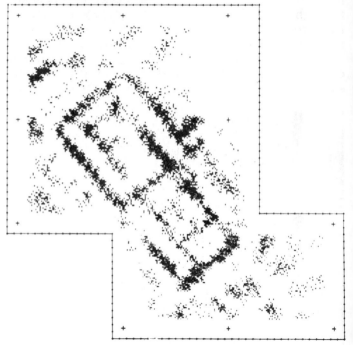

together where possible. Missing pieces are replaced with plaster. Plaster is also used to put together skeletons and other broken objects.

Finding sites from the air
Aerial photography has been useful in finding many new archaeological sites. Photographs taken from the air often show traces of buried buildings that cannot be seen from the ground. An aerial photograph of a wheat field may show a line of taller wheat right across the field. This probably means that someone once dug a ditch there. The ditch is no longer there, but the soil that covers it is more fertile than in the rest of the field.

An earthwork that has long ago been plowed over may be impossible to recognize at ground level. But a photograph taken from an airplane when the sun is at a low angle can show up ridges and hollows, clearly revealed by their shadows.

Buried roads and walls can also be traced in aerial photographs which show lines where plants are shorter than those around them. The thin layer of topsoil over the ancient wall or road means that the plants' roots cannot reach very far into the earth. Their growth is therefore stunted all along the line of the wall.

On the ground

Before archaeologists begin digging a site, they like to pinpoint as many features as possible. Several instruments have been invented for this purpose. One of these is an instrument that measures the RESISTIVITY of the soil. Special meters are used to measure the resistance of the soil to electricity passing through it. Electricity is conducted largely by water in the ground, so well-drained soils have a greater resistance to electricity than less drained ones.

Since buried walls and other objects hold water to different degrees, they can be found by the different electrical resistance of the soil covering them. A meter

on a table with four sharp iron probes as legs is used. The electrical current is passed between one pair of legs. This current spreads through the soil around them and the resistance of the soil is measured between the other two legs. The instrument and its results are shown on the opposite page.

Magnetic fields

Another useful instrument, the proton magnetometer, has been developed to measure tiny changes in

Below left: An aerial photograph reveals the clearly defined outline of an 18th-century house.

Below: The remains of the Roman town of Silchester, England, seen from the air (left). In the infrared photograph on the right, markings which hardly show up in the ordinary photograph stand out clearly. The reds and blues of infrared false color pictures are of great help to the archaeologist.

magnetism. Most soils and rocks contain small particles of iron oxide. Each of these particles has a weak magnetic field. Usually, these little particles are all mixed up and pointing in every direction. Their magnetic fields cancel each other out.

However, if the soil in which they are found is heated above 1300 degrees F (700 degrees C), the particles lose their magnetism. When they cool again, the particles become magnetic once more, but now they are all magnetized in the same direction as the Earth's magnetic field. As all the particles are magnetized in the same way, they act as though they are one big magnet. This stronger magnetic field can be detected by a magnetometer, so archaeologists can find out where the ground has been heated around kilns and hearths.

Pits and ditches that have been filled up also have a slightly greater magnetic field that can be detected. The magnetic particles in these line up with the Earth's field to a slight degree, even without being heated.

Metal detectors are used by archaeologists too, but they are not quite as useful as many people think. In an excavation, metal objects will be recovered anyway, and it is wrong to dig them out before they are placed in their proper order.

Dating methods

For many years the only way ancient cultures could be dated was by the discovery of histories containing lists of kings. But this method was unreliable. The invention of radiocarbon dating in the 1940s was very important for archaeology.

All living things take in tiny quantities of a radioactive substance called carbon-14 from the air. From the moment an animal or plant dies, the carbon-14 in it decays at a regular rate. After about 5700 years, half of the carbon-14 in it has decayed. After another 5700 years half of the carbon-14 that is left has disappeared, and so on. So scientists can tell the age of pieces of bone, wood and other natural materials by measuring the amount of carbon-14 left in them.

Ring dating

After a time, however, it was discovered that the

Above: A fossilized tree has been cut through to show the yearly growth rings.

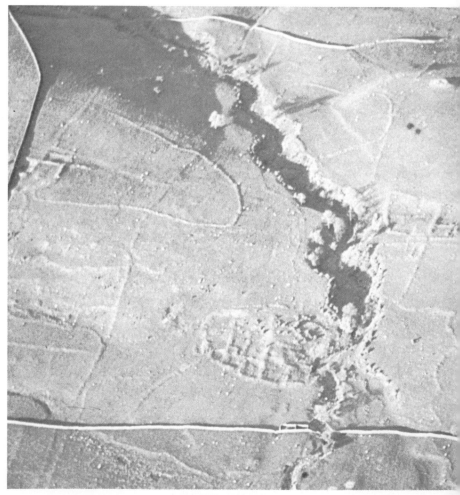

Right: An aerial photograph taken in North Yorkshire, England. The remains of a Roman fort show clearly in the center. Crop marks are also picked out by the shadows. The clump of trees conceals an ancient burial mound. This photograph was taken in the evening to accentuate the shadows.

amount of carbon-14 in the air has not always been the same. As a result, some archaeologists began to doubt whether carbon-14 dating was reliable. Then an American, Dr. C. W. Ferguson, began to study tree rings as a way of dating objects.

Trees grow by adding a fresh ring of wood to their trunk every year. In a good growth year the ring will be a broad one, in a bad growth year, a narrow one. Tree rings can be seen in almost any log of wood. If the life spans of two trees overlap, it is possible to see parts of the same thick and thin ring patterns in each. By cross dating in this way, scientists have worked out a long sequence of wood samples. If the date of any one tree ring is known, the scientists can date all the rings in the sequence. Dr. Ferguson has built up a continuous tree-ring "calendar" dating back to 6100 BC.

It has also been found possible to measure the amount of carbon-14 in each tree ring so that variations in the rate of loss of carbon-14 can be recorded. Then, by comparing the tree-ring information with the results of carbon-14 tests, archaeologists can fix the exact date of objects from any time after 6100 BC.

Telling the age by light

A method of finding the age of pieces of pottery is called thermoluminescence. It was discovered that when pottery is heated to about 800 degrees F (430 degrees C) ELECTRONS are released. These escaping electrons cause a glow which can be measured. The more light given out, the greater the length of time since the pottery was baked. Objects as old as 100,000 years have been dated in this way. As pottery does not contain remains of living things, it cannot be dated by the carbon-14 method.

Underwater archaeology

Water can preserve some materials that would very soon rot away if exposed to the air. Wood and certain fabrics are such materials. So archaeologists are becoming more and more interested in discovering and studying old objects found underwater in wrecks and ruins.

But underwater archaeology is not easy. The early divers were hampered by their heavy helmets and bulky diving suits. In the last 30 years, however, the

Below: Crop marks caused by variations in crop growth are one of the signs of ancient remains that the archaeologist will look for in an aerial photograph. The diagram shows how plants are shorter over the hidden remains of a wall at A. At B, the plants are taller because of the ditch that was filled with rich topsoil. These signs are usually invisible on the ground, but stand out clearly in aerial photographs. The differences in crop heights have been exaggerated in the drawing.

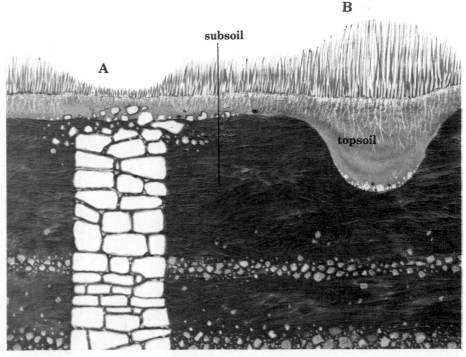

B

subsoil

A

topsoil

Above: When a pot is heated in a kiln, magnetic particles in it line up with the earth's magnetic field, which changes with time. This pot is being spun inside a magnetometer to find out the direction of the original magnetism. When the direction is known, the date of the pot can be worked out.

Above: Thin slices of rock are ground down to a thickness of about a thousandth of an inch (0.03 mm). These almost transparent slices can be examined under a microscope (left). This one shows a tiny section of Iron Age pot. In it are pieces of limestone, and in the center a piece of fossilized seaweed.

development of the aqualung has helped to make the diver more mobile.

When the area of a wreck has been located, divers search it piece by piece so that they cover every foot of sea floor in the area. If they are lucky enough to find and identify the wreck, then the area containing it is marked off, often in the sort of grid pattern used on land.

Much of the underwater archaeologist's work is like that of the archaeologist on land. But the rules of careful digging, recording and labeling are harder to keep. Under the sea, currents and shifting sand can change a site overnight.

One of the most famous underwater finds was the old Swedish warship *Vasa*. The *Vasa* sank in Stockholm harbor in 1627. In 1956 a Swede, Anders Framzen, found the vessel after years of searching. The ship was raised by steel cables attached to floats. Now she stands in a Stockholm museum after months of special treatment to preserve the fragile iron and woodwork. On board the *Vasa*, the bodies of sailors were found with their clothes still well preserved.

Underwater excavation is dangerous work. The team must have a good understanding of the sea floor, ocean currents and temperatures on the site. Divers take turns to work, each staying down for from 12 to 40 minutes, depending on the depth.

One of the most valuable tools for underwater excavation is the airlift. This is a long tube reaching from the surface to the sea floor. A pump on the surface sucks sand, mud and small objects up the tube as the diver clears the site.

Preserving metal objects

Metal objects, except for gold, decay after thousands of years in the ground. The first step in saving them is to scrape off everything that is not part of the original metal "skin." Then the surface is cleaned and, where necessary, repaired. A protective coating of resin prevents further decay. X-ray photographs can reveal decorative designs invisible beneath the decay.

See also: AERIAL PHOTOGRAPHY, AQUALUNG, DIVING, MAGNETISM